Hunting - Fishing
and
Camping

L. L. Bean, the Author, of Freeport, Maine
and Moose shot by him in Fall of 1935.

Hunting - Fishing
and
Camping

BY
L.L. Bean

with a Preface by Leon A. Gorman

APPLEWOOD BOOKS

Distributed by The Globe Pequot Press

Hunting-Fishing and Camping was originally published in 1942.

ISBN: 1-55709-206-0

Thank you for purchasing an Applewood Book.
Applewood reprints America's lively classics—books
from the past which are still of interest to modern
readers—on subjects such as cooking, gardening, money,
travel, nature, sports, and history. Applewood Books are
distributed by The Globe Pequot Press of Old Saybrook,
CT. For a free copy of our current catalog, please write to
Applewood Books,
c/o The Globe Pequot Press, 6 Business Park Rd., P.O.
Box 833, Old Saybrook, CT 06475-0833.

10 9 8 7 6 5 4 3 2 1

Library of Congress Cataloging in Publication Data
Bean, L.L. (Leon Leonwood), 1872-1966.
    Hunting, fishing, and camping / by L.L. Bean.
        p.   cm.
    Originally published: 1942
    ISBN 1-55709-206-0 : $19.95
    1. Hunting.   2. Fishing.   3. Camping.   4. Bean, L.L. (Leon
Leonwood), 1872-1966.   I. Title.
SK33.B42   1993
799—dc20   93-9694

Preface

We are pleased that the *Hunting, Fishing, and Camping* book written by my grandfather, Leon L. Bean, in 1942 is being reissued. In his introduction, "L.L" wrote: "The object of this book is not to bore my readers with personal yarns and experiences but to give definite information in the fewest words possible on how to Hunt, Fish and Camp." True to his word, his book contains 104 tightly written pages including lots of pictures and lots of practical, down-to-earth advice.

"L.L.'s" book sold 200,000 copies and became a classic in outdoor literature. Much has changed in outdoors practices since the original publication, yet much of "L.L.'s" advice is still sound. Most important, however, is what the book and the old-fashioned photos tell us about "L.L.'s" time. It's a window on part of America's real past and an invaluable part of our heritage. We're very proud it's being reproduced for today's outdoors people as it was published fifty years ago.

Leon A. Gorman
President
L.L. Bean, Inc.
May, 1993

Introduction

The object of this book is not to bore my readers with personal yarns and experiences but to give definite information in the fewest words possible on how to Hunt, Fish and Camp.

I am confining the territory to Maine, however, the same instructions and rules apply to all sections of the country where the same fish and game are found.

To make this book just as brief as possible I am dealing only with major information. Minor details are easily learned by practice. The instructions are so condensed that the reading time of the whole book is only 85 minutes.

If you have youngsters coming on, let them read this book. The information is just as important as many school text books.

I am a firm believer in the conservation of all fish and game and the strict enforcement of all game laws. To my mind hunting and fishing is the big lure that takes us into the great open spaces and teaches us to forget the mean and petty things of life. I recommend that duplicate Chapters 3, 4, 14, 15 and 16 in the back of this book, be cut out and kept on your person when big game hunting.

I desire to acknowledge with appreciation the valued cooperation of:

The Maine Forestry Department
Warden Supervisor Arthur Rogers
Henry Milliken   Parker Foss
Henry Beverage   Guy Bean
George Soule   O. H. P. Rodman
J. Larry Hawks

4

Dragging in a 10 point Buck on snow. For dragging in deer on either bare ground or snow see general information on page 13.

Wild deer in natural surroundings. It is very seldom that you would get a shot with rifle or camera as good as this.

Table of Contents

Deer at Salt Lick

When you go deer hunting don't expect to find deer as tame
or as plentiful as shown in the above pictures.

Chapter 1
Deer Hunting On Bare Ground

 The first thing to decide: Where shall I go? Second: How many do I want to make up the party?

Where to go is the most important question to settle. You will find your answer on page 77.

Now for your party. A perfect trip may be ruined by one person who does not fit. I recommend small parties, not over four. Two makes a good party.

The next thing after making up your party and where to go is to decide on your camp. Shall you use a tent, a lean-to, an old logging camp or go to a regular Sporting camp?

A Sporting camp is the most comfortable and the least trouble, but sometimes the hunting is not so good on account of too many hunters.

This picture shows that if you do not keep a sharp lookout you may walk right by a deer that is within easy gun shot.

Next is your equipment and what to wear—you will find your answers to both these questions on pages 29, 30 and 31.

Now that you are settled in camp, each hunter should look over safety rules and make a copy of signals in Chapter 14.

The next question is: How are you going to hunt? With a small party I recommend still hunting as driving is out of the question. I realize that driving is fairly successful in the Southern States but not in Maine. I have found still hunting the most successful method on both bare ground and snow. Early in the season you stand a chance to get a good shot near camp. The best hunting is early in the morning, regardless of the season. The first thing to do is to find out the direction of the wind. Travel with the wind in your face. Walk slowly, stop often, take in all the territory around you and always be in a position to shoot quickly.

Watch for fresh signs and try to follow the way you are going but always keep the wind in your face, if possible.

Do not hunt too long the first day or two. Start back to camp by 10:00 o'clock. The middle of the day is the poorest time to hunt. If you find fresh signs near camp go out again about 2:00 o'clock and sit down in a place where you have a good view and an open place to shoot.

If it is a beech-nut year you will do well to put in a lot of time on the beech ridges. You are very likely to find where deer have pawed over the beech leaves looking for nuts. Walk very slowly along where

Pursued by dogs, this doe ran out on the ice of East Lake, where she fell. Deer cannot walk or run on glare ice. State Game Warden, Supervisor Arthur Rogers, conveyed her to the State Game Farm.

A nice 10-point Buck shot on bare ground.

you can see quite a distance. If it is a bright, clear day keep near the edge of the ridge where the hard wood and black growth meet. If you find fresh signs sit down where you can see some distance looking into the wind. If you are not sure of the direction of the wind wet your finger in your mouth and hold it over your head. The side that feels cold is where the wind is coming from.

If there are no beechnuts look for signs on burned ground and where lumbermen have operated. Deer browse on small hard wood shoots and raspberry bushes. Whenever you find signs keep a sharp lookout and step where you will not break twigs. Deer's eyesight is poor but their sense of hearing and smelling is very keen. They are very apt to scent or hear you and be off before you see them.

If you wound a deer and find blood do not rush him. Signal your partner. Sit down and wait for the deer to lie down and stiffen up. If in the afternoon, however, get him before you are obliged to leave for camp if possible as it may storm during the night and obliterate the trail.

Chapter 2
Deer Hunting On Snow

Strike out, taking your easy walking gait, until you hit a fresh track. Walk right along on it until it begins to zig-zag, then you must stop, look and listen.

Mr. Deer is looking for a place to lie down. Now start hunting in earnest. Walk slowly and always be in a position to shoot. See that there is no snow in your sights or in your gun barrel.

If you get a standing shot, take a very careful aim at the fore shoulder if possible.

Should you suddenly come on to running tracks you can walk as fast as you like until deer starts walking again. Then slow down and watch for zig-zag tracks. Always keep a sharp lookout on both sides of tracks as occasionally other deer come in from the side.

If deer starts browsing note the direction of the wind. If the wind is not in your face, start circling so as to bring it in your face. Because you are wasting your time by following a deer that can scent you before you see him.

The white spot on this deer indicates the best place for your first shot.

For successful hunting the snow should be soft, dry and fluffy. If the snow is crunchy under your feet or is frozen and crusted, it is worse than no snow at all for good deer hunting.

It takes a little practice to determine the difference between fresh tracks and old tracks, but if snow falls during the night and you are out early in the morning it is fairly certain that you will strike a fresh track if there are deer in the vicinity.

Chapter 3   How To Dress A Deer

First swing him around so that his head will hang over a small log or nubble with hind quarters down hill. Spread his hind legs well apart, make a careful incision in the belly right where it curves up from the legs, cutting through the skin and the very thin layer covering the paunch. Remembering that the hide and membrane is very thin here and that you do not want to cut into the paunch. Place the point of your knife between the first two fingers of your left hand, so that the back of the hand will press the paunch down and the point of the knife will cut the skin. Cut forward until you have an opening from twelve to fifteen inches long. Roll up both sleeves above the elbow, insert both hands, one on each side of the paunch, well forward and roll it out through the opening. Do not make this opening any larger than is necessary in order to do this. The bowels and liver will follow the paunch. Now reach way forward with your right hand and you will strike a membranous wall. Puncture this with your fingers and on the other side you will find his heart and lungs. Reach beyond this and cut windpipe with jackknife. Now pull out the heart and lungs and you have a deer that is known as "woods dressed". It is not necessary to cut the throat to bleed him. In most cases all the blood will escape through the shot hole. If not, the dressing operation will bleed him thoroughly. It is a good idea to remove the end of the intestine at the rectum. By doing this you will make a drain. By drawing a small bough through this hole all the blood will drain out.

Chapter 4   How To Hang Up A Deer

If a small one you will have no trouble as you can tie your drag

Showing how one man can hang up a large deer.

line around his neck, throw the loose end over the limb of a tree and pull him clear of the ground.

If a big deer, find a sapling that can be pulled over, so that, you can hitch your line to it high enough, so that, when it springs back it will lift the carcass from the ground. In case the "spring back" is not enough, use a pole with crotch or fork at end to prop it back in place. In some cases two poles are much better than one. Now sign and detach tag from your hunting license and fasten it to the deer.

Photo—Courtesy Maine Development Commission

Fill out the tag that is attached to your hunting license and fasten it to your deer. In Maine, deer are subject to seizure if not properly tagged. (See page 88).

If deer is hung in the open, arrange black growth boughs, so the sun will not shine on it.

The next thing is to spot (blaze) trees and bushes from where it is hung to the nearest travelled trail or stream that leads to camp.

Do not depend on your memory as to where the deer is hung. Many a deer has never been found after it was hung up. Should you employ a guide, he will do all this work, but, in place of a gun insist that he take along a medium size axe, a small camp kit with tea and lunch enough for 36 hours, (see Chapter 38). If you want to get pictures have him take along a camera. Your own rifle is enough but if you want to get partridge he can take along your light shot gun.

The most difficult and back-breaking task connected with deer hunting is the process of transporting a deer to camp. If the deer is small and there is snow on the ground, you can do fairly well by fastening a rope to the neck or antlers of the deer and attaching the loose end to a piece of sapling about 1½ inches in diameter and six inches long, using the sapling as a handle. If you have a companion, use a handle two feet in length.

Dragging a big buck on bare ground for several miles is a task that you will long remember. Get all the members of your party to help you.

If you kill a deer "way back" and can hire someone with a horse to transport it to camp, you certainly are in luck, because the few dollars that you spend for toting will save you much hard labor.

A drag line with turned handle is much easier on the hand than a piece of sapling.

Photo—Courtesy Maine Development Commission

Dragging out a large deer is not an easy job. (See Chapter 4).

Chapter 5   How To Hunt Black Bear

No game animal in Maine is more elusive, more difficult to stalk, or once having been started, more difficult to shoot than a black bear. A bear is seldom caught unawares, for he has an almost uncanny sense of smell and is faster than chain lightning in his mental and physical reactions.

In northern Maine the best month to hunt black bear is October, for it is the month that they are locating comfortable winter quarters and are intent on piling on surplus fat in anticipation of a long sleep to come.

Photo—Courtesy Maine Inland Fisheries and Game Dept.

Black Bear is the most difficult game animal in Maine to shoot but with a little experience not hard to trap.

If the beechnuts are plentiful, walk slowly along the hardwood ridges, not on the top of the ridges, but where the black growth mingles with the hardwoods. Travel with the wind in your face. Be on the alert. Should the bear you are hunting smell or hear you, he certainly will head for parts unknown without any preliminary motions. He won't stop to investigate, and once started, you might as well find a needle in a haystack as to attempt to locate him that day.

If you find the leaves of beech trees in small stacks or windrows and signs look fresh, sit down in a well hidden spot and keep on the lookout. Stay there a half-hour or so and then proceed on your way along the edge of the same ridge. Look carefully at the "black stumps" as you walk along, for occasionally these "stumps" are black bears.

If there is any place where there has been a forest fire and con-

Bear traps must be enclosed in a hut and plainly labeled.
(See page 88).

sequently acres of blackened trees and stumps, walk along the edge of such places. Bears like to explore for grubs and you may see one ripping a stump apart for just such morsels.

One of the most successful bear hunters in Maine confines his activities to the vicinity of lumber camps. The place where the camp's garbage is thrown away is carefully looked over. If signs denote that bears make frequent forages on the garbage the hunter climbs into a tree near the spot and awaits the visit of Bruin. He hunts only in the afternoon, climbing into his tree perch about two o'clock and

Large black bear in trap.

staying there until dark.

Bears like to walk up and down old tote and logging roads, so saunter along slowly and sit down occasionally—and trust to luck. Black bear hunting is mostly a matter of luck anyway. You may hunt for twenty years and not catch sight of one, or you may see one the first day on a hardwood ridge.

You must be a good rifleman indeed to hit a running bear. In full flight he looks like a rolling barrel and he travels much faster than you would think him capable.

Chapter 6
How To Hunt Moose

The same safety rules, equipment and wearing apparel for deer hunting apply to moose hunting.

At this writing, moose are protected in the State of Maine and in

This is a very unusual picture of a Bull Moose charging, taken by Warden Supervisor Arthur Rogers, Waterville, Maine. Note hair standing up on back of neck. I do not want to give the impression that Moose or any other wild animals in Maine are dangerous. (See page 88).

New Brunswick, Nova Scotia and Prince Edward Island, Canada. The other eight provinces have open seasons.

There are several methods of hunting moose but if you have never been moose hunting I suggest that you employ a guide. It takes much practice to call a moose and the average man should not attempt without excellent assistance.

The outdoorsman who uses a camera can enjoy some real sport if he is in a locality where moose are plentiful. Wait until there is snow on the ground, pick out the tracks of a cow moose and her calf, and then slowly trail the animals. If you are careful and the wind is blowing in your face, you stand a good chance of seeing at least one moose. Moose are curious, and will often stand and watch you approach within shooting distance with your camera.

Bringing in a large Moose head for mounting.

Chapter 7
How To Hunt Ducks and Geese

 Present restrictions make duck and goose hunting much more difficult than it was a few years ago when you could use live decoys.

For ducks I recommend a 3 shot 12 guage Automatic Shot Gun. Use a long range load with number 4 shot.

I use about fourteen removable head decoys. Make your set about 100 yards off a point of land in an open spot with grass enough around so that you can scull quite close without ducks seeing you. When you see birds coming keep very still until they light in. Lay very low in your gunning float until you are within range. Don't try to kill the whole flock. Pick out the nearest duck and stay with it until it drops before trying for a second bird. Go where wild rice is plentiful if possible and get your decoys out by daylight. The Federal law now allows shooting sunrise to sunset.

A gunning float all dressed up for action. When sculling ducks it is important that float be camouflaged.

If you are obliged to hunt where there is no grass or wild rice, construct a blind of boughs, old brush or other natural objects just out of reach of high tide and set your decoys within easy shooting distance. Keep all of your belongings out of sight so that your blind will look natural. Cover your boat with seaweed if possible or beach it where it will not be conspicuous.

L. L. Bean's Duck Hunting Camp at Merrymeeting Bay near Brunswick, Maine.

Photo—Courtesy Maine Development Commission

Left to right: A guide, L. T. Patterson, the author's son, Warren Bean and guide with a nice bag of Black Duck shot at Merrymeeting Bay, Maine.

L. L. Bean with his duck gun, practicing on clay pigeons, so as to be ready for the duck hunting season when it opens.

Goose hunting is so difficult you can not expect success without a guide. There are two very important things you should attend to before you start hunting for either ducks or geese and that is: **1st.** Learn to hit a flying target. If there is no trap shooting field where you can go, get an inexpensive hand trap and practice with your duck gun until you can break about 50%. **2nd.** Your cap, coat, pants and boots should blend with the duck marsh surroundings. I recommend olive green or khaki.

Unless you learn to hit a flying target you are very apt to stop your gun on a flying duck and shoot way behind it. I have been with hunters, before live decoys were prohibited, who had good chances all day long without killing a single duck.

(Always keep in mind the safety rules in Chapter 13.)

Photo—Courtesy Maine Development Commission

A good dog comes in handy to retrieve your ducks.

Chapter 8
How To Hunt Ruffed Grouse

The ruffed grouse, more commonly known as "partridge," is found in every section of the State of Maine. It is probably more abundant and more widely distributed here than anywhere else in the country. The bird is found deep in the big woods and in covers only a short distance from towns and cities.

Most hunters prefer to use a good dog when hunting Ruffed Grouse.

There are two kinds of grouse in Maine—smart and foolish. The latter are so tame that they can be shot on the ground or on the limbs of trees with a pistol or rifle. These are the birds found in the big woods. They are identical in every way with those found in the settled areas except that they have no fear of humans.

The grouse of the inhabited sections are much smarter than their backwoods brethren. We don't shoot them with rifles or pistols; we don't always hit them with a shotgun. They have been well-termed "the smartest upland game bird that flies."

We Maine hunters look for grouse in farming country. We expect to find them in alder and birch thickets, around the edges of fields where berries are plentiful, under wild apple trees, on the oak ridges in acorn years, even in the softwood growths. But we also know we are likely to find them where least expected. There are more than fifty different kinds of food eaten by these birds and finding them is a matter of finding food sources, and, of course, suitable cover.

In the early part of the season we frequently find the birds in flocks of three to six. Later on in the Fall, singles and pairs are more common.

While most hunters prefer to use dogs the birds can be hunted successfully by "walking them" up, as we say. But this requires fast shooting.

Photo—Courtesy Maine Development Commission
A bird dog is not absolutely necessary when hunting Ruffed Grouse.

Although grouse are more abundant during the first part of the season than the last, many hunters prefer the last two weeks for hunting. That is because the leaves are off the trees and one has a much better chance to see, and hit, these fast-flying birds. They are also likely to be found in more open country, in old apple orchards for example, than during the early part of October when there are many more kinds of food available.

However, one who plans to hunt grouse in the northern part of the State of Maine will find the birds more plentiful the first part of the season. The flocks are thinned out rapidly in most of the sections that can be reached by automobile. In the settled areas, in the central and coastal counties, the kill is more evenly distributed through the six weeks of hunting.

One of the best ways to hunt ruffed grouse in the wilderness sections of Maine is to walk slowly along old tote and logging roads. If you flush a grouse and don't get a shot, be on the alert as there probably will be at least one or two additional birds in the vicinity.

Either a .20 gauge or .12 gauge Shotgun will serve your purpose. If you use a double, load one barrel with a No. 7 shell and the other barrel with a No. 6 shell. Use the No. 7 when you shoot at birds nearby, and No. 6 at longer range.

Learn to shoot "on the wing." If you are a fair skeet shooter, you will get your share of the ruffed grouse that you flush, especially where the "territory" is open. Learn to "lead," this knowledge is gained by practice at skeet shooting or using a hand-trap.

When you kill a ruffed grouse, examine the contents of its crop. That will give you an idea as to what the birds are feeding on, and you can then hunt in the vicinity of the places where such food abounds.

Photo—Courtesy Maine Development Commission

**Taking time out for lunch and rest after bagging
a couple of Grouse.**

Chapter 9
How To Hunt Woodcock

No state in the country offers better woodcock hunting than Maine. The birds are found in all of the coastal counties, in the central section and to some extent in the north. In addition to the thousands of woodcock that breed and raise their families in our birch and alder thickets all of the New Brunswick and Nova Scotia birds cross Maine on their Fall migration to the southern wintering grounds.

The heaviest concentrations of woodcock are undoubtedly in the expansive covers of Washington County in the eastern part of the state. In the early part of October native birds are found in almost every birch and alder stand. The coastal part of Hancock County also affords excellent shooting. There are many large covers in that section of the state; areas so large that a hunter can spend the better part of a day in one cover.

One day's bag limit of four Woodcock.

In the central and western parts of Maine the hunting, for the most part, will be in smaller sections. For example, there are at least twenty productive woodcock covers within a half-hour's drive from the L. L. Bean Factory in Freeport. Lincoln, Knox, Waldo and parts of Kennebec County also afford excellent shooting, mainly in covers that hold from four to a dozen birds at the beginning of the season; more when the flight is underway. Many of these are large enough to accommodate a hunting party of four; others can best be hunted by two men.

The first week of the open season (usually the first of October) may be the surest time to find an abundance of woodcock in Maine. One is sure of finding native birds in the coastal and central sections.

As every veteran woodcock hunter knows it is not possible for us to predict the flight movements; the migrations are guided pretty much by weather conditions. Normally, however, the heavy migration will be about the middle or last of October.

Hunters who have their own dogs and who know woodcock covers when they see them, will have no difficulty in finding good shooting during the Maine season. Since the hunting period is set by Federal authorities it is not possible for me to give the dates in this book. In recent years, however, the period has been in October.

A copy of the Federal migratory bird regulations, issued annually in August, and available from the Fish and Wildlife Service in Washington, D. C., will provide the dates, bag limit, and all other data on the woodcock season.

Chapter 10
How To Hunt Pheasants

Maine pheasant hunting is confined to the coastal counties, these birds being unable to withstand the deep snow in the northern sections during the winter.

Like grouse, the pheasants are found in the farming sections and around the outskirts of villages. In many cases they frequent the same covers and it is not unusual to find pheasants in woodcock covers.

During the first part of the open season we look for them in fields and covers that contain seed plants or weeds. We also find them in gardens from which corn, beans and other foods have been harvested. They also feed on berries and apples but not to the extent that grouse do.

Later, after they have become wise to ways of men, dogs and guns the birds are more likely to be found in thick cover and in softwoods. A cover so thickly grown with vines and bushes that it is nearly impenetrable will be a favorite hiding place for pheasants.

The State of Maine liberates four or five thousand mature pheasants every spring. These birds breed in the wild and produce flocks ranging from four to a dozen. In addition, the State liberates six to seven thousand nearly full grown birds in the latter part of the summer. These supplement the wild stock and are available for hunting in the Fall. Although they are not so plentiful as grouse and woodcock there are enough pheasants in Maine to provide good sport. They are an added reason for late season grouse hunting since the open seasons run together the first two weeks in November.

To any who have not hunted pheasants let me add this warning: The birds are smart, fast-flying, and not easy to kill. Many of the shots will be at ranges over twenty-five yards and in many cases the birds will rise out of gunshot. When wounded they will sometimes elude a top-notch retrieving dog.

It is also possible to combine duck hunting and pheasant hunting in some sections, devoting part of the day to each species. That would be especially true in the coastal areas of Maine where tide is an important factor in hunting waterfowl.

Anyone contemplating hunting pheasants or any other Maine game species should, however, check seasons and regulations in the Maine hunting law handbook, issued annually and obtainable from the Department of Inland Fisheries and Game, Augusta, Maine.

PUZZLE—Find five pheasants. This is a photograph, taken by the Author, of a flock of eight wild pheasants. The camouflage is so perfect that only the cock birds show.

Chapter 11
Hunting Equipment

All modern Rifles not smaller than .25 Calibre are O. K. for deer hunting. I personally use a .25 Calibre Automatic Remington which carries six shots. Regardless of the kind of gun you buy, do not change too often. Once you get a gun you like, stick to it. You can do much better shooting with a gun with which you are accustomed.

Although I have used the same rifle for years, I continue to use up all my old shells practicing just before starting on my hunting trip. I want to be sure that the sights are O. K. and that the gun is in perfect working condition. I also buy new shells each season as I have known smokeless powder shells to miss fire. Old shells are O. K. for signaling.

I do not use a regular cartridge belt or clips, instead I carry ten shells in a small zipper leather case that loops onto my belt. Besides the six shells in my rifle, I distribute twelve more in my coat pockets. (28 in all)

There are many days you will not use a single shell but if you wound a deer you are likely to use quite a few and he may take you so far from camp that you will need many more for signaling. (See page 34).

I carry two compasses, one on my wrist and one Hunter case in my

Always make sure that your sights are O. K. and that your rifle is in perfect working condition before starting on your hunting trip.

pocket. (See Chapter 15 "How to Use a Compass")

For other small equipment I carry about twenty matches in a small sealed waterproof container for emergency use only. Also other matches for daily use. One medium size pocket knife, one sheath knife or small belt axe, a vest pocket flashlight, a few strips of celluloid or small fire kindler and a small pocket waterproof game bag in which I carry a lunch. Also, drag line about 8 ft. of strong window cord is good for hanging up and dragging out deer.

If you do not have a guide make your equipment just as light as possible. If you do have a guide See Chapter 38.

If you are going to camp and do your own cooking, you will find grub lists in Chapter 33. I suggest that you choose food that is easy to prepare, especially so if you can go to the door of your camp with an auto.

If your party is more than two or you plan to stay more than six days you will need to increase the amount proportionately.

Non-residents in Maine can not camp and kindle fires from May 1 to December 1 in the open without a registered guide for every five members of your party, except at public camp sites. (See page 88). A copy of either the Game Laws or Fishing Laws may be obtained by writing the Fish and Game Commissioner, Augusta, Maine.

Moose eating lily pads and roots. They will put their head way under water to get bottom vegetation in bogs and ponds.

Chapter 12

Wearing Apparel

As I have been quite a successful deer hunter for the past thirty-one years (shooting 32 deer) I am taking the liberty of recommending just what I wear.

Shoes: One pair 12" Leather Top Rubbers. I also take along a pair of 6½" Moccasins to wear dry days on the ridges before snow comes.

Stockings: Two pairs knee-length heavy woolen and two pairs light woolen.

Underwear: Two union suits same as worn at home.

Pants: One pair medium weight all wool with knit or zipper bottom. Also wear from home your heaviest business suit.

Coat: One medium weight, all wool, red and black with game pocket in back.

Shirt: Two medium weight, all wool; one to be red plaid in case you go out to drag in deer without coat.

Cap: A reversible red on one side for deer hunting and brown on the other side for duck hunting.

Gloves: One pair of light weight woolen with leather strips on fingers.

Handkerchiefs: Six red bandanas. Do not use white in woods. I also recommend colored toilet paper.

Miscellaneous: One pair heavy Suspenders, one heavy Belt, one very light weight Sweater or Wind Breaker, one Silk Rain Shirt, one Pajama Suit, two Towels, a few Toilet Articles, and one pair Slippers. Coming from a long hunt change to slippers and light stockings. This is important to keep feet in best condition.

For deer hunting I believe it is very important to wear partly red coat and cap but if you don't care to go to the expense, pin a red handkerchief over cap and one on back of coat to avoid accidental shooting.

Some old hunters do not wear red because they believe that it frightens deer. This is a mistaken idea.

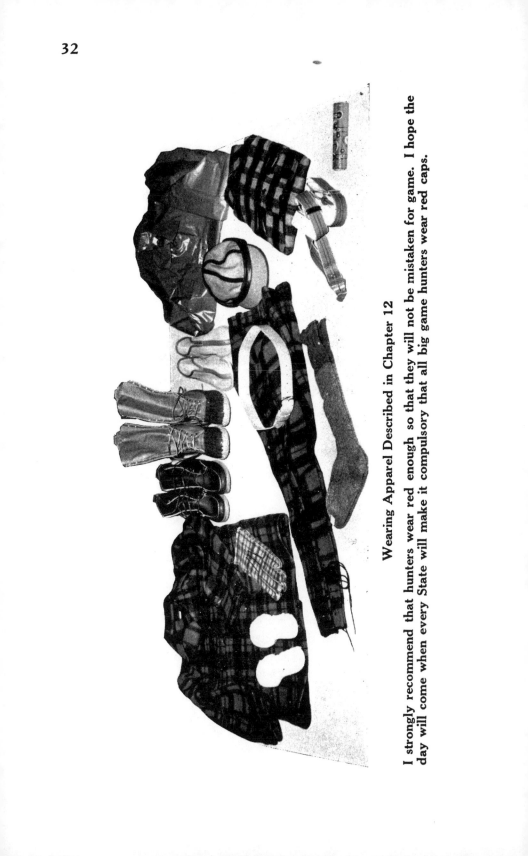

Wearing Apparel Described in Chapter 12

I strongly recommend that hunters wear red enough so that they will not be mistaken for game. I hope the day will come when every State will make it compulsory that all big game hunters wear red caps.

I have always worn red and have proof that it does not frighten deer but even if it does, who wants to take unnecessary chances with his life?

These recommendations apply only where car or boat takes you to camp door. If camp is located where you are obliged to walk or canoe quite a distance, I recommend that you wear hunting clothes from home. Also eliminate some other articles that you feel you can get along without.

Chapter 13
Safety Rules

Never have a loaded gun in camp. Load and unload your gun outside with muzzle pointing away from camp. Leave your rifle in camp with the chamber open.

Never point your gun, loaded or unloaded, in the general direction of another person.

Do not shoot at anything until you are positive it is not a person. **Always** keep your safety on when in company with another hunter.

Never pull the trigger just for fun.

Never shoot at bottles or other hard surfaces from which a bullet may glance.

Always look to see if a gun is empty before handling it.

Always put gun through a fence, muzzle first, before climbing through.

Never carry a loaded gun in a car. In many States, including the State of Maine, it is unlawful.

Never pull a gun, by the muzzle, from a boat or automobile.

Do not violate the Fish and Game Rules. (Co-operate with your Game Warden by reporting any violations that come to your attention. The Warden treats this information strictly confidential).

Every big game hunter should know how to build a fire in a rain or snow storm.

A hunter, with plenty of matches, froze to death in a snow storm near one of my camps through the fact that he was unable to build a fire.

Personally I always carry a few ounces of fire kindler and when out in a bad storm occasionally build a fire for practice as follows:

1st. Gather plenty of dead, sound branches from black growth trees (pine is preferable) and plenty of bark from white birch trees.

2nd. Scrape the snow off an open spot on high ground and brush it clean with fir boughs.

3rd. Lay down any paper you have, fire kindler and small strips of bark.

4th. Add very small dead, sound limbs and a few pine whittlings.

5th. Light the fire kindler and add small pieces of limbs as fast as the flames will take them.

6th. Keep adding small wood until coals begin to form. You now have a fire that will take large, sound, deadwood even if it is quite wet.

Chapter 14
Signals for Hunters

It is very important that you have a system of signals that every member of your party will recognize. I recommend the following: When you want to get in touch with another member fire two shots about five seconds apart. Anyone of your party hearing it will reply with two shots. You answer with one shot. He immediately starts looking for you. After traveling ten minutes he will fire one shot and you will answer with one. When he believes that he is near you, he will "Hello." Not receiving an answer he will fire one more shot which you will answer with one. Continue this one shot conversation until you are within hailing distance. After calling for help and receiving a reply **do not** leave your position.

Chapter 15
How To Use A Compass

There is no excuse for getting lost if you carry a good compass and know how to use it.

Camping places are invariably located on trail, tote road, stream, lake, telephone wire, etc. We will say that your camp is on a good sized stream or well defined road running North and South. You cross the stream or road and hunt to the East for several hours. When you want to go to camp all you need to do is travel West. Hold compass so needle arrow points to "N" then pick out some object in a due West direction and go to it. Keep repeating this and you are sure to hit your road but it may be a mile or more below or above your camp. You are out of the woods anyway and if you have been over the road a few times you will soon see land marks that will tell you which way to go.

Lakes, old railroads, telephone wires, etc., always run in some general direction and you must be sure of this direction when you start out and always be sure which side you are hunting on.

Before starting out I usually get someone in the party to help make a rough sketch of the territory and always carry it with me. A rough map of this kind is a big help to find the very shortest way to camp.

At times you will feel sure your compass is wrong. The best way to overcome this feeling is to carry two compasses. In checking one compass against the other, place them eight or ten feet apart and away from your gun or other metal. Another reason for carrying two compasses is that one might get broken. In fact, compasses have been known to get out of order. When compass needle swings back and forth several times and finally settles in the same direction on two or three tests it is O. K.

Photo—Courtesy Maine Development Commission

A good sized stream, near camp, is a great help in the use of a compass.
When crossing note carefully the direction it runs. If it runs from North to South and you cross it going West, when you are ready to return to camp simply travel East and you are sure to hit this stream.

This man, who was caught in a snow storm without snowshoes at Little Joe Mary Lake (snow 5 ft. deep), found a dry cedar where the heart had been burned out in a forest fire, fixed a pair of Skis and got out safely.

Chapter 16

How To Find A Lost Hunter

In case one of your party does not show up at camp when night falls as has previously been his custom, do not get excited and do not do a thing until 6:00 P. M. If you start signaling before 6:00 P. M. other hunters who have not gotten into camp are likely to butt in and make it very misleading.

Eat your supper and see that the lantern is full of oil. Then go outside with rifle, lantern and flashlight. At exactly 6:00 P. M. fire two shots. Listen a moment for a reply. Not hearing any, walk about one-quarter mile and repeat your signal. If you get a reply, see a fire or note any odor of smoke, continue the signals, always walking in the general direction that you believe your man is located.

In the meantime what is the "lost" hunter to do? If, in the late afternoon, he realizes that he is lost or so far from camp that he can not get in, he selects a sheltered spot where dry wood is handy, starts a fire and collects a lot of wood before dark. At exactly 6:00 P. M. he listens for a signal. On hearing it, he answers and the signals continue the same as in the daytime. Hearing no signal he wastes none of his shells but pounds a signal at regular intervals with a club on a sound, dead tree. If there is no dead tree available, select a live tree and peel off a spot of bark where he wants to pound.

In the morning, if not sure of the direction to camp, he is not to leave the spot or to shoot except to answer his party's signals. Keep a smoke going and pound out a few signals about every ten minutes.

The party at camp should not stay out too late. Notify a Game Warden or Sheriff during the night and continue the search at daybreak.

By following these simple rules the lost hunter or his party have nothing to worry about.

(It is a good idea to mark all trails a short distance each side of camp. Lay down small limbs of black growth with broken end pointing toward camp. Your party can do it in less than an hour.)

Chapter 17
How To Fish For Salmon, Trout And Togue

Of all the fresh water game fishing, Salmon is my favorite. They hit hard, jump high and fight every inch of the way to the net.

During the first month after the ice goes out in the Spring I find

Fishing party with Salmon and Trout caught at Moosehead Lake 1939. Over half of these fish were taken on Live Bait Fly as described on page 40.

Left to right: Dr. A. L. Gould, Willis Libby, Levi Patterson, and L. L. Bean

Salmon and Trout are considered the best game fish in the State of Maine.

Pictures show a large male Salmon and two nice square tail Lake Trout.

Togue look the same as trout except they have a crotched tail.

Male Salmon invariably have a hooked lower jaw.

When you get a strike where there are both trout and salmon you can usually tell at once which fish you have hooked. Salmon will jump whereas trout will stay under water or just break the surface.

trolling with bait the most successful. I use a sewed-on Smelt on **one** rod and Night Crawlers on the other. I recommend a 7½ **ounce** 9½ ft. Trolling Rod, level winding 100 yard Reel, 25 lb. test **Nylon** Line with markings at 50, 75 and 100 ft., a 15″ Leader, two **Swivels** and a 12″ Snelled 2/0 Hook. Row slowly and run from 50 to **100** feet of Line until you land your first fish. Note how much line **you** had out and continue using the same length.

For sewing on smelts and shiners I recommend the **following** method: Place a few gut hooks in can of water or minnow bucket **so** snell will be pliable when ready to bait up.

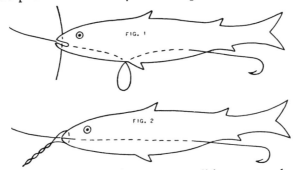

1st.   String minnow lengthways on snell by passing hook through mouth, out at belly then right back through same hole and out **at** side as shown in Fig. 1.

2nd.   Draw snell tight which takes out loop and forces snell **to** pass straight through minnow as shown in Fig. 2.

3rd.   Stick point of hook into side of minnow between the **two** tail fins.

4th.   Close mouth with little wire as shown in Figs. 1 and 2.

5th.   Crowd minnow back into hook so as to form a bend.

6th.   Wind twisted wire around snell twice and try trolling at **side** of boat. Bait should turn to imitate wounded minnow. If too **slow** put in more bend. When satisfactory, wind balance of wire **around** snell and you are ready to **fish.**

The little wires cost only 15¢ for a tube of fifty.

After the first month I run a live bait fly, as illustrated below, on one rod and a sewed-on minnow on the other. A shiner hooked through the lips as shown will keep alive for about two hours. Do not stick tail hook into minnow. I use a 5½ ounce Fly Rod for the live

bait fly. Later in the season when it gets warm and the fish go into deep water it is much more difficult to get them to take a surface bait. Many times it becomes a question of going home empty handed or resorting to a somewhat unsportsmanlike method of deep trolling.

Fishing party taking time out for lunch at Sebago Lake, Maine. Left to right: Dr. Arthur Gould, Walter Dumser, Charlie Manchester and L. L. Bean.

For deep trolling you need a very stiff rod, a solid 150 yard reel and metal covered 100 yard line. Use a set of spoons size 2 to 6/0 according to the depth of water with plenty of swivels. Run sewed-on minnow on one rod and night crawlers on the other. Use a short snelled 2/0 hook without leader so that bait is not over 8 inches from tail spoon. Keep a few hooks soaking in bait pail as it is about impossible to sew on minnows with a dry snelled hook.

Always carry a rule of some kind to be sure fish is legal length. When returning fish to water wet both hands and use a hook disgorger.

Trout and togue are caught in the same way as salmon except you

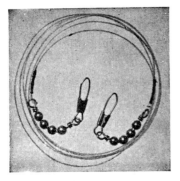

When trolling with spoon use plenty of swivels.

troll a little slower and fish a little nearer shore for trout and farther away for togue.

Do not strike your fish too quickly. Strip off a few yards of line so as to give it time to get bait and hook well into its mouth. This is important and applies to both trout and salmon, the former especially are very slow taking in bait.

I have recommended a metal covered line which I prefer but any line which tests thirty-six pounds or more is O. K. Fly fishing is explained in Chapters 22, 23, 24 and 25.

Chapter 18
How To Care For Minnows And Worms

Minnows and worms for bait need to be kept fresh and lively. For minnows on short trips I recommend a puckering string, canvas bucket with an inside wire cage. On warm days place a piece of ice on top of cage under puckering string. On cool days or after ice has melted, dip bucket in water often enough to keep canvas damp. Water should be changed about every hour. When in camp remove cage and submerge in cold water.

On long trips I recommend a large bait pail with removable inside cage. Place a piece of ice on top of pail in such a way that the steady drip-drip-drip from it into the pail will supply an artificial means of injecting oxygen into the water and keep it cool. On arrival at your destination remove cage and submerge in cold water.

Angle worms and night crawlers should be packed in moss in a good size tin container with a few holes punched in cover. Get an eight quart galvanized pail, put in a large piece of ice and place container of worms on top. Then cover pail with old piece of damp cloth. Renew ice as needed. When bait fishing I see to it that my minnows and worms have very careful attention.

There are two kinds of garden angle worms, light and dark. The dark worms are much better as they keep fresh and lively much longer than the light worms.

Night crawlers and angle worms can be kept all winter in a wooden box filled with damp moss, in the cellar.

A little oatmeal, coffee grounds or cornmeal makes good food. Feed them every few weeks.

They come in handy for early fishing when the ground is too frosty to dig.

Chapter 19
How To Fish For White Perch

Use a bait casting rod. A Number 1 hook will be O. K. Angle worms are all right for bait. If you use a float, adjust it so that the hook will be about three or four inches from the bottom of the lake.

If you fish without a float, use a small sinker, pinching it to the line six or eight inches above the hook. Let the bait sink slowly. When the sinker hits bottom, raise it nine or ten inches and keep it there for a couple of minutes. Raise it slowly and make another cast.

If you are fishing on a lake where white perch are known to be plentiful, and you don't have any luck, paddle your canoe or row your boat to another section of the lake and make several casts. If this isn't successful, try another and still another spot. When you do catch a white perch, stay in the vicinity because they are "school" fish and you may catch a dozen or more as fast as you can lower and raise your baited hook.

Just at dark is the best time to fish. At certain seasons they will take a fly at this time of day. Use your regular fly rod and wet trout flies, as shown on page 56, with a little lead "twiston" on your leader. Let fly sink well under water and retrieve it slowly.

When they are taking a fly you will get them faster and have a lot more sport than with bait.

If there is an old log dam at the outlet of the lake or pond you are fishing, try your luck in the deep-hole just below the dam. It is a good place to fish at the opening of the season.

L. L. Bean's well stocked Private trout pond in Freeport, Maine, where fly rods, reels, lines, leaders and flies are tried out.

Chapter 20

How To Fish For Black Bass

Pound for pound, Black Bass are the gamest fish in Maine.

The season opens late. In Maine, bass can not be taken with bait before June 21st. However, three per day may be taken with fly from June 1st to June 20th. If you have never done fly fishing for bass you have missed a lot of fun.

During the first of the open season (June 1st to July 10th) I use flies. Later when the water gets warm, bass feed on or near the bottom and will notice bottom activities more quickly than disturbances on the surface.

A comfortable fishing boat and a nice Black Bass.

Live minnows and frogs are excellent baits for bass fishing. A minnow three inches long is large enough. If you use frogs, choose the small ones. Hook minnows and frogs through both upper and lower lips, pointing hook upward under lower jaw. Start fishing immediately after hook is properly set.

For equipment a rod of medium stiffness, 9 feet long will prove satisfactory. Line should be of 15 lbs. test. Sinkers should weigh about one ounce.

If worms are used, those that are clean and bright will prove most satisfactory. Use a No. 1 or No. 2 hook with gut snell. Put the worm on corkscrew fashion so that about half an inch of the worm projects below the point of the hook. When completed, no part of the hook should show.

You can often get a bass to take artificial bait by trolling with colored minnow or a red and white plug.

A very enjoyable day may be had by making up a picnic party. Your Guide will take along everything necessary for a bass chowder. All you have to do is catch the bass and meet at a prearranged camp site. Bass makes the best chowder of any fish that swims.

Picnic Party

Chapter 21
How To Fish For Small Brook Trout

This is an inexpensive sport enjoyed by a large number of fishermen right near their own homes. It is practically all bait fishing. Angle worms are about the only bait used in Maine.

I recommend a 9 foot telescope steel rod, an inexpensive level winding reel, a 25 yard, hard surfaced line, an eight-inch snelled No. 2 hook and fairly large sinker.

Most trout brooks are very bushy and many times you will find trout in the most difficult places to fish.

This is where your telescope rod comes in. By telescoping it up to four or five feet it makes it easier getting through the bushes and into the hole you want to fish.

Do not use a small, soft line, as it snarls so easily you will spend most of your time unsnarling it from brush and bushes. An old level fly line makes an excellent line for brook trout fishing.

When fishing in a still pool do not yank too suddenly. Give the fish time to get bait well into its mouth.

I carry my worms packed in moss in a bait pocket in my coat. On warm days I occasionally dampen them with cold water. Take plenty of worms so that you may change bait often as trout will take a wiggly worm when they will not take a dead one.

Place a few leaves or moss in the bottom of your creel before putting in your first trout and continue to do so with each trout you catch.

When bait fishing for small trout on a pond with boat or raft, let the bait sink slowly until sinker hits bottom. Then raise about a foot. Hold it there for one or two minutes before making another cast. Do not yank too quickly. Once you have located fish do not leave the spot until you are sure they have stopped biting.

Note recipe for cooking trout on page 70.

Here is a stream pool where a fly can be used. Most trout streams are too bushy to use a fly.

Follow directions in our book and this will not happen.

Chapter 22

Fly Fishing—General

You may have read or have heard that fly fishing is an art that requires expensive equipment and the mastery of many difficult tricks. Perhaps you have neglected this part of fishing because you have considered the sport hard to learn. But you certainly won't learn to fly fish if you don't try. The more casts you make the better you will understand the technique. Don't attempt at first to make casts of 60 or 70 feet like many experienced fly fishermen do. Most fish are taken within 35 or 40 feet of the angler.

Although dry fly fishing is faster than wet fly fishing, you can use dry flies to advantage only at certain periods of the year. For early fishing in the Spring you probably will depend on bait fishing. Then comes wet flies and later, dry flies. (Regardless of the lure you use during the early part of the season, or the variety of wet or dry fly that you employ later on, you will get a strike occasionally, that is only natural.)

There are often times when both occupants of a canoe can fish successfully, but as a rule there should be but one person fly fishing from a canoe. After you have enjoyed an hour's sport, change seats with your companion and let him fish.

If you are on a lake that you are not familiar with, let your companion paddle slowly parallel to and about 100 feet from the shore. Fish to right and left. If you don't get a strike, try again about 200 feet from shore. For bass and pickerel, make your casts as near the shore as possible among the water plants.

When you use a wet fly, allow plenty of time after you make a cast so that the fly will have a chance to sink several feet. Retrieve it slowly so that the fly will be agitated.

48

Always use a net when taking a fair sized fish from the water.

If it is the right season for dry fly fishing, I suggest that you paddle along slowly until you see a fish rise to the surface for food. Then start fly fishing. If you are fishing with wet flies and see a fish leap to the surface, change to a dry fly and try your luck in the vicinity of the action which you have just witnessed. Always use leaders that are well soaked and pliable.

Whatever type of rod, reel and line that you use, it is a good idea to use a heavy line with a heavy rod, and a light-weight line with a light-weight rod. (See chart on Page 52). Don't make the mistake of using your fly rod as a derrick to lift a caught fish into the canoe, because nets are made for that purpose.

There are many and varied artificial attractions for wet and dry fly fishing. It is well to take along a practical assortment of flies in your tackle box, as well as several leaders of various lengths.

If you are contemplating buying a fly fishing outfit for wet and dry fly fishing, the first thing to be considered is the rod. If for wet fly fishing get a medium action. If for dry fly fishing a stiff action. If for both wet and dry a medium stiff action. Personally I do not care for a soft action rod for any kind of fishing. A rod 8½ or 9 feet in length is about right. If it is 8½ feet long it should weigh approximately five ounces if constructed of split bamboo.

The next thing to buy is a reel. I like a single action reel with a capacity of about 50 yards of line.

A good fly line is essential. As most of your casts on trout streams will average less than 40 feet, it is not necessary to have a line more than 25 yards in length. You may prefer a tapered line, or perhaps a level line. I prefer a Bug Taper Line for all kinds of fly fishing.

Auto Rod Carrier—is a safe, handy way to carry rods on short trips from home, also from stream to stream and pool to pool. Can be attached to car in 2 minutes.

This is a matter of personal choice, and after a few seasons of trout fishing you will find that you are constantly experimenting in lines, reels, flies and other equipment.

You will also need a tube or bottle of fly dope to keep the midges and mosquitoes away and a pocket knife, with hook hone set in handle, also hole in bolster for shaping hooks.

Chapter 23   Fly Casting

Actually there is no such thing as fly casting. It's the line that's cast and not the fly. The fly simply rides along as a passenger. Keep this in mind and you will soon learn how to cast. In bait casting the lure carries out the line but in fly casting the line carries out the lure.

The caster in Fig. 1 is ready to begin; Right foot forward, right thumb parallel on the handle; left hand grasping the line which lays out about thirty feet in front on the water.

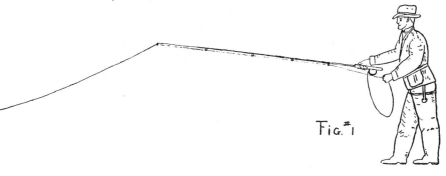

Fig.#1

Starting the back cast, the left hand is brought slightly back to sraighten out the line and at the same time lift the rod slowly to the 10:00 A. M. position and without hesitation, "snap" the rod back to the 2:00 P. M. position still grasping the line in the left hand which now travels slightly up. The line has now left the water and is flying back in a wide arc. Give it time to go back straight as shown in Fig. 2.

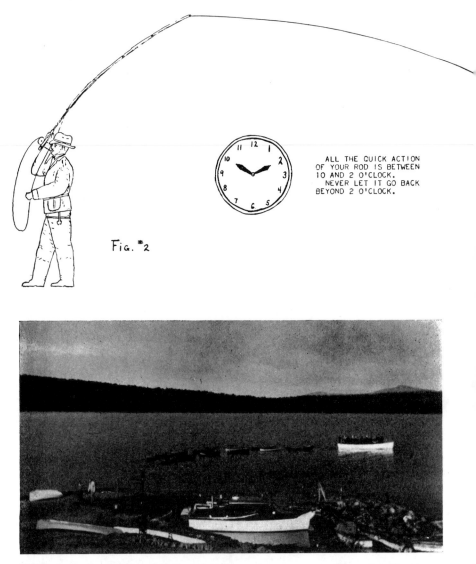

ALL THE QUICK ACTION OF YOUR ROD IS BETWEEN 10 AND 2 O'CLOCK. NEVER LET IT GO BACK BEYOND 2 O'CLOCK.

Fig. #2

Fishing party, with guides and string of canoes, starting for Spencer Bay, Moosehead Lake, Maine. On reaching their destination each guide will take one or two fishermen in a canoe.
(The Author's Cabin Boat in the foreground.)

The rod has now reached the 2:00 P. M. position in Fig. 2 and the line is parallel to the water. The forward cast is started by "snapping" the rod forward to the 10:00 A. M. position and releasing the line from the left hand at this point. The fly will strike the water in front of the leader and your cast should produce results.

Properly executed the cast should follow the pattern shown in Fig. 3 and that's all there is to fly casting. From here on perfection depends on practice.

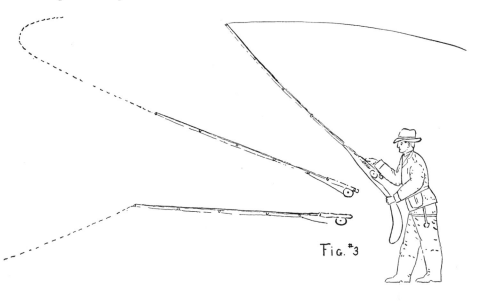

Fig. #3

Common Faults Of The Beginner

Fault No. 1—Trying to pick up a crooked line from the water. No perfect cast can be made unless the line is straight at the start.

Fault No. 2—Starting the "snap back" at the 8:00 A. M. position instead of the 10:00 A. M. position.

Fault No. 3—Not giving the line time to straighten out on the back cast. This is a difficult fault to correct. Try changing your position by putting the left foot forward so you can swing around and watch the line straighten out behind you. After a little practice you will notice a slight pull as the line straightens out.

Fault No. 4—Bringing the rod back beyond the 2:00 P. M. position. This causes the spring to leave the rod, and the line, when started, will pile up. Try to imagine you are going to throw a potato from the tip of your rod.

Fault No. 5—Releasing the line from the left hand before the rod reaches the 10:00 A. M. position. This also causes the line to pile up.

Fault No. 6—Trying to cast too much line. The longer the cast, the more difficult it is. Fish are caught at from thirty to forty feet in stream fishing. No need for a long cast here.

Fault No. 7—Casting "stiff arm." Every advantage should be taken of the leverage in the forearm and wrist. This leverage can only be had when the elbow is near the body. One well known instructor recommends placing a bottle of "Scotch" under the right arm during practice.

Fault No. 8—Lunging and thrashing. Remember your line, leader and fly only weighs a few ounces and no brute strength is necessary to throw this weight. Fly casting is a sport that requires rhythmic coordination between mind and body. It can only come through practice and patience. It is difficult to see your own faults, so it might help if you had a friend read these instructions, then coach you.

To get the best results with your fly rod it is important that you have the proper line. After much research we recommend line sizes as follows:

Rod Length	Rod Weight	Medium Action Rods		Bug Taper	Stiff Action Rods		Bug Taper
		Level	Taper		Level	Taper	
7½′	2½-3½ ozs.	E	HDH	HDH	D	HDH	HCH
8′	3½-4½	D	HDH	HBH	D	HCH	HBH
8½′	4½-5	D	HCH	GBG	D	GBG	GAG
9′	5-6	C	GBG	GAG	B	GAG	GAG
9½′	6-7	B	GBG	GAG	B	GAG	GAG
10′	7-8½	B	GAG	GAG	B	GAG	GAG
10½′	8½-10	B	GAG	GAG	B	GAG	GAG
11′	10-12	B	G2AG	GAG	A	G2AG	G2AG
12′	12-14	A	GAG	G2AG	A	G2AG	G3AG

Chapter 24

Fishing For Brook Trout With Dry Flies

Walk slowly upstream. If you see a large pool ahead, approach it carefully. Do not stand so that the sun will cause your shadow to fall on the trout's haunts. Make as little noise as possible.

Make your casts so that the fly will land lightly on the water, for you are attempting with artificial lures to attract trout that are accustomed to natural food which they have in abundance during the Summer. Casts of 25 or 30 feet are easier to make and usually will produce more trout than long and difficult casts.

Changing Flies

Always be ready for a strike. You must set the hook instantly when fishing with dry flies for brook trout, because the little fellows are gifted with the ability of sampling your attraction and discarding it about as fast as you can wink an eye. Large brook trout have a tendency to "bore down" with a fly and you have more time to set your hook properly.

Do not allow the fly to sink. Don't create a disturbance by jerking a fly through or under the water. Your business is to interest a trout enough for him to leave his resting place in an eddy, or behind a rock or sunken log.

Brook trout lay headed upstream, on the lookout for natural food. It sees anything that is in front or at a quartering angle. It is useless to cast behind a trout.

Use flies that look "alive." When it hits the water it should not look like a dead insect.

Although you will find that you will have better luck fishing upstream, it is not unusual to fish downstream to good advantage when conditions warrant same, and this is a matter which demands personal judgment.

If you are on a fairly wide stream and you see a pool that looks good, wade slowly out and make frequent short casts. If you are on a stream that has been fished hard, it is often a good plan to sit down occasionally near the largest pools. Enjoy your pipe and watch for the rise of a trout, for when you see one there is an incentive to the sport. You know that it depends on your own ability to inveigle the little fellow again to the surface.

The Author with two nice salmon taken on live bait-fly.
(See Page 40).

Chapter 25

Fly Fishing—Flies and Lures

Lake Trout and Landlocked Salmon. Streamer flies prove efficient in either shallow or deep water. The flies that I have found most effective in the following order are: Supervisor, Red and White Bucktail, Gray Ghost, Golden Witch, Edson Tiger Light, Edson Tiger Dark, Lady Doctor, Parmacheene, Bolshevik, White Bucktail, Brown Bucktail. For trolling I recommend live bait fly as shown on page 40.

Bass. The following flies are okay for bass fishing: Col. Fuller, Parmacheene Belle, Scarlet Ibis, Montreal, Brown Hackle, Gray Hackle. Try a small spinner with these flies. Take along a fly rod mouse and give it a trial when other lures fail.

Pickerel. A small spoon and a bright fly is excellent for pickerel. A white and red, or a yellow and red fly with weedless attachment is preferable. Often a small spinner with a piece of pork rind will prove effective.

Atlantic Salmon. For Atlantic Salmon the six flies that I have found most effective in the following order are the Jock Scott, Dusty Miller, Silver Grey, Black Dose, Silver Doctor and Durham Ranger. For early Spring or high water fishing the larger size hooks are the best, and I recommend size 1, 2, and 4 single hooks, and size 2 and 4 double hooks. For low water or very clear, single hook size 6, 8 and 10, double hook 6 and 8.

Brook Trout. For early spring fishing large trout flies are generally the most effective such as the Parmacheene Belle, Silver Doctor, Royal Coachman and White Miller. Also at this time trout will take Nymphs fished near the bottom. As soon as the water drops and becomes warmer the darker and smaller patterns are recommended such as Brown and Grey Hackle, Montreal, Cowdung and Black Gnat.

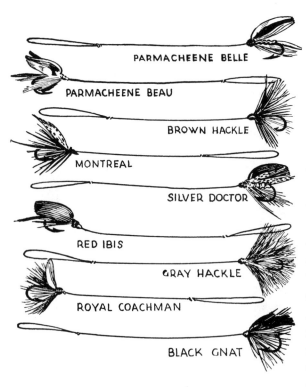

PARMACHEENE BELLE
PARMACHEENE BEAU
BROWN HACKLE
MONTREAL
SILVER DOCTOR
RED IBIS
GRAY HACKLE
ROYAL COACHMAN
BLACK GNAT

As soon as natural insects begin to appear in numbers that is the time to change to the Bivisibles and dry flies which will take fish through the warm summer months.

Chapter 26
Camping—How To Choose A Tent

When you purchase a tent, get one that is not too large or too small. When you decide on size, type and weight, you must take into consideration the number of people in your party and the method of transporting your outfit and supplies.

Two adults are enough to house in any tent with the exception of an extra large one, although a tent of medium size will often accommodate two adults and one or two children.

For general camping there are three styles of tents which are the most useful, these being the wall, the so-called umbrella or marquee, and the cruiser's or hiker's model. Each has its purpose.

I recommend the wall tent if you can handle its transportation. One large enough to accommodate a camp stove is the most desirable.

For added comfort a canvas floor and fly are well worth taking along. The fly will offer protection against sun and rain, and the floor will keep the inside of your tent cleaner and warmer. Removable floor is the best, because it can be taken out and cleaned.

Two practical tents with deer in yard. This is a Summer scene. However, don't expect to find deer in your front yard after the season opens.

Umbrella tent showing bobbinet door.

Hiker model tent.

The umbrella tent is popular with motor-campers, and most campers prefer the poleless type with sewed-in floor. It requires but little space when packed and is easy to erect. Buy one that is equipped with curtains for they provide ventilation which is so necessary during the warmer months of the year.

The hiker's model is all right for canoe and hiking trips where weight and space is at a premium. A tent of this type is easy to erect and take down. Choose one with a sewed-in floor of canvas.

Chapter 27
Camping—Selecting A Camp Site

When selecting a place to erect your tent, make certain that you are near good drinking water and ample fuel.

Remove rocks and tree limbs from the space you select to set your tent. Don't pitch your tent among large trees, especially trees that are rotten.

Choose a place where water will run away from the tent as much as possible. After your tent is erected, dig a small trench around it about three inches deep close to the sidewall. Dig trenches at right angles to the main trench about three feet long and four inches deep to take care of the rain.

See Chapter 36 regarding excellent camp sites in Maine made possible by the Maine Forest Service. Many of these camp sites are located in good hunting and fishing territory, have well-built rock fireplaces and sheltered tables and benches.

Chapter 28

Camping—How To Erect A Tent

Erecting a tent is a matter of practice. The Cruiser's or Hiker's model is the easiest to erect. Stake down the corners of the floor, adjust the pole and guy lines.

If you use either a Wall tent or an Umbrella tent, I suggest that you erect it in your own back yard previous to a camping trip, so that you will get the "feel" of putting it up correctly.

To erect a Wall tent 9½ feet wide and 12 feet long:

First: Drive five stakes down three feet apart.

Second: Opposite and parallel to the stakes, drive another row of stakes, having the two rows about 21 feet apart.

Third: Unroll the tent and stretch it out on ground between the two rows of stakes.

Fourth: Attach guy lines loosely to the proper stakes.

Fifth: If the poles are jointed, put the ridge pole in and then one section of the back pole and front pole and repeat the process until tent is up.

Sixth: Peg down all four corners.

Seventh: Adjust guy lines to remove slackness.

It may be necessary to move the stakes holding the guy lines either toward the tent or away from it, and if so, remove only one or two stakes at a time while making adjustments.

To erect the poleless type Umbrella tent.

First: Open up your tent and secure all corners of the floor with tent pegs.

Second: Put the top spreading frame together and lay it inside on the floor.

Third: Using one of the corner poles, shove top spreading frame in place, letting the bottom of the pole rest in center of tent.

Fourth: Adjust one corner pole and then the opposite one.

Fifth: Put the third pole in place, remove the pole from the center and put in its proper place at corner.

Sixth: Adjust poles to remove slackness.

Seventh: Outside guy ropes should then be attached to stakes and the canopy poles placed in position.

Eighth: Put canopy up and attach side curtains.

Ninth: Drive all stakes holding guy ropes straight down, not on an angle.

Loosen the guy ropes a little and adjust corner poles if it starts to rain.

When camping or fishing in June you stand a chance of seeing a young fawn deer as shown above. Note how the spots blend with the leaves so as to make almost a perfect camouflage. Do not take these fawns from the woods. It is illegal to disturb them.

Chapter 29

Camping—In Old Lumber Camp

There often is good hunting and fishing in the vicinity of abandoned lumber camps, and if the camps are in fair condition a little time and labor is all that is necessary to make at least one of the camps habitable.

Choose one of the smaller buildings for your abode—it probably will be the office because it usually is in the best condition.

As the roofs of the camps are often poor, it is advisable to take along a heavy tarpaulin or a tent fly so that you will have a makeshift roof.

You may be lucky and find an old box stove in one of the camps, but the chances are you won't, so it is a good idea to carry along a small folding stove and telescoping stovepipe.

Take along a handful of nails of assorted sizes, plus a small roll of stovepipe wire, because you will always find such items useful in making an old lumber camp habitable.

You will find good drinking water in the vicinity due to the fact that all lumber camps are constructed near a spring, stream or lake.

This is a picture of an Old Lumber Camp which with a little work makes a comfortable camp.

Chapter 30
Camping—How To Build A Bough Bed

Cut two logs seven feet long and six or eight inches in diameter, and two logs five feet long and six or eight inches in diameter. Place the two seven-foot logs parallel to each other and nail the two shorter logs to their ends, making a rough pen to hold boughs. If you haven't nails in your kit cut some pegs or stakes about eight or ten inches long and drive a peg into the ground on each end of each log close to the outer edge, so that the log can't roll outwards when pressure is exerted from within.

Cut some good-sized fir or spruce boughs with your axe. Load the bunk with them. Point all the butts downward into the earth. Then cut a bushel or more of very small fir balsam boughs. Your sheath knife will do the trick.

Lay the small boughs very carefully on the bunk, starting at the head of the bed. Lay them almost on end, with the under side up.

You will probably run out of boughs by the time you are two-thirds down the bunk, but if the bed is soft and springy under your shoulders and hips you will sleep okay. If you have plenty of time, cut enough small boughs to finish the bed.

This is a poor picture of an Old Lumber Camp office which with a little work makes a comfortable camp.

Chapter 31   Camping—Equipment

The best hunting and fishing is often found away from the "beaten trails." What to take to those far-back places depends on the number of people in the party, the duration of the trip, the time of the year and the methods of transportation.

If you travel by Shank's Mare to such locations, or go by canoe, take only the necessities. The list below is intended for two people.

1. Hiker's or cruiser's tent.
2. Two sleeping bags.
3. Large canvas knapsack.
4. Packbasket with waterproof cover.
5. Small axe and sheath.
6. One two-cell flashlight with two extra batteries and one extra bulb.
7. Folding reflector baker.
8. Gasoline lantern. (Take candles if transportation is difficult.)
9. Utensils for cooking and eating should include frying pan, three-quart stew pot with cover, small coffee pot with strainer spout, one stirring spoon, one baker tin, two tin plates, two spoons, two knives, two forks, two cups, salt and pepper shakers.

Auto Camping Equipment

The following list of equipment for auto camping is for two people. If there are more people in the party, you will naturally need more equipment.

Check these items when you pack your equipment in your car at home.

1. Tent and stakes.
2. Two folding cots, or two sleeping bags, preferable equipped with air mattresses. Camp cots are cold and uncomfortable without mattresses, especially during the early fishing season and late hunting season.
3. Air-bed pump.
4. Strong folding card table.
5. Two camp stools.
6. Two reclining camp chairs for relaxation purposes.
7. A two-burner gasoline stove and a two-gallon safety gasoline can.
8. Two blankets per person if cots are used.
9. One gasoline lantern. A lighted gasoline lantern resting on the floor of your tent for an hour is ideal for taking off the chill during Spring and early Fall camping.

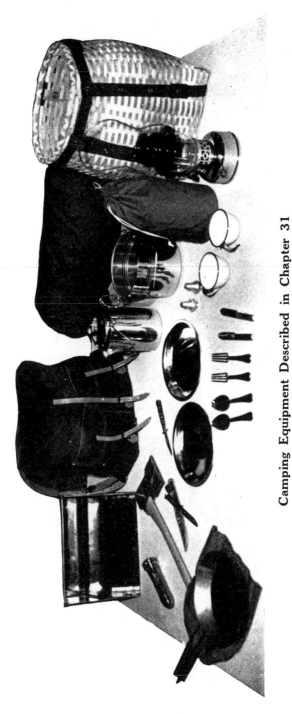

Camping Equipment Described in Chapter 31

Be sure to select your camping equipment carefully. Take only practical, necessary items and check them off as you put them in your car.

10. Cooking and eating utensils should include a heavy guage 3-quart coffee pot with strainer spout; a 4-quart pail; a medium-sized frying pan; two 2-quart covered pots; reflector baker; long-handled fork; salt and pepper shakers; knife, fork, spoon, cup and plate for each person; one large spoon; one knife with at least an 8-inch blade for cutting meat; one long-handled spoon and one cooking spatula.

11. One camp axe with sheath.

12. One small mattock for digging trench around tent.

13. One flashlight with extra batteries and extra bulb.

14. A few nails and a small roll of stovepipe wire will be found useful around camp.

Chapter 32
Camp Cooking—How To Use Reflector Baker

A reflector baker is one of the most useful equipment items that you can take along on your hunting, fishing and camping trips.

Cooking with a reflector baker is easily learned. If you use the baker outdoors, build a small fireplace or "pen" of stones or green logs. I prefer stones. Select stones about eight or ten inches square that are as flat as you can get in the vicinity, and build a small pen having sides, back and top. Two or three thin stones will suffice for the top, and you may be lucky enough to find

Reflector Bakers come two models, non-collapsible as shown above and collapsible shown below.

one stone that will do the trick. The little pen should be 12 or 14 inches high, 18 inches deep and 12 inches wide.

If you can't find suitable stones for constructing a makeshift fireplace, make one of green logs, splitting those for the top so that your cooking pots will set level.

Build your fire in the fireplace. Place the reflector baker about four inches from the front, so the blaze hits the bottom and reflects upward, also the blaze hits the inside top and reflects down, and you can bake anything that can be baked in an oven. You can regulate the heat by moving the baker.

If you use any type of wood-burning stove that doesn't have an oven, place the baker against the side of the stove, as close as possible. With a bit of experimenting, you can use a reflector baker in conjunction with a gasoline stove.

It is possible to bake beans in a reflector baker without interfering with your other duties around camp if you use a wood-burning stove. Lacking a bean pot in your outfit, use a two-quart pail or dish. Soak the beans overnight, and in the morning place in pail, adding two tablespoons of sugar, teaspoon dry mustard, very little salt and pepper, and nearly one pound of salt pork. Now fill pail with water, place on shelf of baker, and place baker against side of stove.

Ordinarily, half a pound of salt pork is sufficient to use in baking two quarts of beans, but you will find that a pound is better if you are away from camp most of the day and can't attend to your cooking properly. If you plan to be away from camp all day, fill the stove with wood before you leave camp. When you return at night, start your fire and add water to the beans. Add more water before you go to bed. Beans should be well done for one of your meals the next day.

In most states there are public camp sites where fireplaces are all built. (See page 75).

Chapter 33   Camp Cooking And Grub Lists

It is difficult to state just what any party should carry into the woods for a fishing, hunting or camping trip. Camper's tastes vary, so there must be some leeway as far as grub lists are concerned, and the method of transportation must also be taken into consideration. Naturally, if you are on a canoe or hiking trip far from grocery stores, you must plan your grub list accordingly, making it light in weight and as compact as possible. On the other hand, if you travel right to your camp door in your auto, you can take along a larger variety of foodstuffs and forget the matter of weight and bulk.

I wish to have it understood that the following suggestions, grub lists and recipes are subject to individual correction. When you look at a list of food to be taken on a trip, eliminate the items which you don't like and substitute other food materials of equal weight. For instance, if you like coffee and not tea, don't take the tea along just because it is on a grub list.

May I suggest that you pack food supplies carefully before leaving for camp. Pack such items as flour, bacon, salt pork, sugar, oatmeal, rice, beans and cornmeal, in small bags of medium-weight cloth that are equipped with puckering strings. The individual bags should then be placed in slightly larger bags that are waterproofed. The bags may be tagged so that they may easily be identified.

Food Bags.

The use of dehydrated foods for camping use is rapidly becoming more popular. Dehydrated vegetables are vegetables with all moisture content removed—they crackle and break in your hand.

Such vegetables as beets, carrots, potatoes, onions, turnips, beans and tomatoes are easy to carry in such a concentrated form. Many of the small packages weigh only 1¾ ounces yet the contents will be found sufficient to make several servings. Such vegetables, being in concentrated form, require no refrigeration.

If you go on overnight trips away from your main camp, don't load yourself down with grub. If there are two in the party, take some sandwiches, 1 package Dehydrated Potatoes, 1 package prepared Pancake Flour, 1 can Evaporated Milk, 1 pound Bacon, ¼ pound Brown Sugar, a handful of Coffee, 4 Tea Bags, 8 lumps Sugar, ¼ pound Butter and 4 Doughnuts. This is enough grub for three meals.

Carry a combination salt and pepper shaker, a folding handle frying pan, a two-quart pail, 2 knives, 2 forks, 2 spoons, 2 plates and 2 cups. Put all food and cooking and eating utensils in a small knapsack. The total weight of knapsack, cooking and eating utensils and food supplies is less than nine pounds. By using two knapsacks and dividing the load you can hunt or fish going and coming. If hunting, cover knapsack with red handkerchief.

On overnight trips don't load yourself down.

If you are going hunting, fishing or camping and want to do as little cooking as possible, the following grub list will serve your purpose. It is just about right for a party of two adults for six or seven days. It is for those campers who have an opportunity to easily transport their supplies to camp.

4 Loaves Bread	1 Can Tomatoes
2 Cans Baked Beans	1 Lb. Cornmeal
2 Cans of Corned Beef Hash	4 Ounces Salt
1 Lb. Coffee	4 Ounces Soda
¼ Lb. Tea	2 Lbs. Salt Pork
2 Lbs. Sugar	8 Lbs. Potatoes
1 Bottle Pancake Syrup	1 Can Peaches
2 Packages Prepared Pancake Flour	1 Lb. Butter
3 Cans Evaporated Milk	1 Small Can Pepper
2 Lbs. Flour	1 Small Bottle Vinegar
3 Lbs. Bacon	1 Small Jar Mustard
1 Lb. Oatmeal	1 Dozen Doughnuts
1 Doz. Fresh Eggs	1 Lb. Cookies
1 Can Corn	

The above grub list may be changed to suit your particular requirements. For instance, some campers make pancake syrup from brown sugar or from cakes of maple sugar.

The flour will be found useful for preparing gravy and for cooking fish. If you plan to be away from camp at lunch time each day, add at least two loaves of bread to the above grub list. Add meat to this list to suit your requirements.

Apples, oranges and other fresh fruits always go well in camp.

Chapter 34
Camp Cooking—Recipes
Venison Steak

Cut steak about 1½ inches thick. Remove excess fat and wipe clean and dry. Have a very hot fire and when frying pan is smoking hot drop steak into the pan and allow to sear quickly on one side. Then turn.

If you like steak medium or well done, reduce the heat of the fire and turn occasionally until at desired stage. If you prefer a rare steak, it will require 10 to 12 minutes; if medium, 15 to 20 minutes.

Serve on a hot platter. Spread steak with butter and add salt and pepper to taste.

Venison Cutlets

Cut small slices of meat from the loin about 1¼ inches thick. Sprinkle with salt and pepper and brush with melted butter. Roll in bread crumbs. Fry in butter.

Roast Duck

Clean and dress duck. Steam about 1½ hours before roasting. Stuff with sliced onion or apple. Sprinkle with salt and pepper and cover breast with several slices of salt pork. Bake about 20 minutes in very hot oven, basting every 4 or 5 minutes with the fat in pan. Remove stuffing before serving.

Roast Leg of Venison

Cut leg and a piece of the loin which will weigh about 5 or 6 pounds. Wipe dry with a damp cloth. Sprinkle lightly with salt and pepper and roll in flour. Attach several strips of salt pork or bacon. Put in roaster and bake three hours.

Photo—Courtesy Maine Inland Fisheries and Game Dept.

Warden Bert Duty serving fried Partridge Breasts at his camp on Roach River.

Fried Grouse

Skin and dress the grouse. Remove the legs. Cut breast in half lengthwise. Break down flat the piece containing the breast bone, doing this with a camp axe or back of a hunting knife. Wipe with damp cloth. Fry in pork or bacon fat. Season to taste with salt and pepper when served.

Roast Pheasant

Dress and clean pheasant. Tie several pieces of fat bacon on breasts. Bake 30 to 50 minutes, basting frequently with fat in pan. Remove bacon before serving.

Pea Soup

Place one cup of split peas and ham bone in kettle and cover with water. Let simmer until peas and meat are well done, this requiring about three hours. Remove the bone and strain peas. Remove bits of meat from bone and add to soup. Thin with milk if too thick. This is enough for four people, one generous serving each.

Brook Trout

Cut heads off. Clean and wipe dry. Fry out liberal amount of pork fat. Roll in flour with a little salt added. Drop in fry pan when fat comes to a boil. Turn often to avoid burning. Fry slowly until every trout is crisp and well browned.

Place in hot platter on clean paper to absorb fat. Have cut lemon on table for those who want it.

(Pork fat is much better than bacon fat or butter and flour is much better than meal).

Camp Style Bean Soup

Put one cup of beans in water and soak overnight. Drain and add two cups fresh water. Pare and dice two medium-sized potatoes and one medium-sized onion and add to pot. Chop fine ¼ pound of salt pork and fry until brown and then add this to the pot. Salt and pepper slightly. Place pot on stove and boil for an hour.

Camp Potatoes

¼ lb. salt pork
8 medium sized potatoes
4 medium sized onions

Fry the salt pork in frying pan until crisp. Remove the pork. Dice. the onions and fry until soft. Dice the potatoes, add onions and cook in covered pan until done. Remove the cover and brown. Add the cooked salt pork after chopping very fine. Do not stir. Turn when brown on the bottom. Salt and pepper to taste. Quantity enough for one meal for four hungry campers.

New England Johnny Cake

½ cup meal
1 cup flour
½ cup milk
1 teaspoon soda (rounding)
1 teaspoon salt (level)
1 tablespoon sugar or molasses

Mix soft. Grease pan, spread evenly in baker sheet and bake until done.

Pancakes

Add 1½ teaspoons baking powder and ½ teaspoon salt to one cup flour. Sift twice. Add milk to form medium batter. Add one egg. Mix well and fry on hot pan. Grease frying pan lightly. This recipe suitable for one meal for two people. (Prepared Pancake Flour requires no baking powder or salt).

Pancake Syrup

Add one-half cup of water to one cup of brown sugar. Boil for fifteen or twenty minutes, remove from stove and cool. When cool, place in bottle or jar for future use. If maple sugar is available, take alone a few cakes. Add 50% water and boil for about 15 minutes.

Camp Dessert

Mix ½ cup of powdered sugar and 1 cup of butter. Add 2 cups sifted flour. Roll this quite thin, cut in squares and bake.

(Try this simple recipe at home).

Chapter 35
Camping Hints

If you take a trip away from the main camp for a day or two, and use either a small tent or a lean-to for shelter, take sugar in lump form, because if you drop some on the ground it is easy to pick up.

If you use a large wall tent or one of the umbrella style, and transportation of equipment and supplies is not too difficult, take along single camp cots for each occupant. A two-burner gasoline stove will be all right for camp cooking. And don't forget the gasoline.

A small alarm clock is an asset at any hunting camp.

For real warmth and comfort on the outdoor trails, a sleeping bag is hard to beat. They are excellent on hunting, fishing and camping trips where it is not practical to carry along folding cots, mattresses

Porcupines are quite plentiful around old logging camps in Maine. Keep your supplies where they cannot get at them.

and blankets. During the summer a piece of cheesecloth sprinkled with kerosene or fly spray is necessary to cover the canopy to keep the black flies, midges and mosquitoes away. If you haven't an air mattress it is a good idea to build a bough bed and place your sleeping bag on it if you desire a real "woodsy" and comfortable bed.

When you get home from a camping trip, take your tent out of its bag and spread it out to dry before storing it away for the winter.

If you lunch along the highway be sure to pick up all rubbish. If you have a fire put it out with water.

To remove rust, soot and grease from pots and pans, wet a cloth in hot water, dip into wood ashes and scour the utensils by a back-and-forth rubbing motion.

When mosquitoes and black flies are plentiful, I recommend stockings long enough so that the pant legs can be tucked inside. This will save you a lot of discomfort.

Chapter 36
How To Prevent Forest Fires

In 1941 about 31% of the forest fires in Maine were caused by careless smokers and campers.

The fire hazard in Maine with its 16,270,000 acres of forest land has become a serious matter.

Maine issued 163,641 hunting and fishing licenses last year (1941). This army of hunters, fishermen and campers can be a great help to prevent forest fires.

In 1941 forest fires in Maine burned over 40,353 acres. The opportunities for recreation, sport and other out-of-door activities, as

offered in certain sections of this State, will no longer be available if fires are allowed to claim their heavy toll.

To help check this yearly loss, hunters, fishermen and campers should observe and put into practice a few simple forest fire protection rules as follows:

1. Rake away all inflammable material before lighting the fire.
2. Don't toss your match away—break it in two, step on it, and be sure it is out.
3. Don't throw cigarette butts from an automobile window.
4. Never build a fire against a log, tree or stump.
5. Never leave a fire burning or try to kick it out.
6. Pour plenty of water on your fire, or use plenty of dirt.
7. When you think it is out, feel of it with your hands to make sure. (A fire is never out until the last spark has been extinguished).
8. If a fire gets beyond your control, call the nearest Fire Warden or Lookout Station.

Maine now has about 200 camp sites made possible by the Maine Forest Service where natives and non-residents may kindle fires

Photo—Courtesy Maine Inland Fisheries and Game Dept.
Poling canoe on dry land at Mud Pond Carry Tramway.

without penalty or without being accompanied by a registered guide. (They are for temporary use. See page 88). Parties using these sites are requested to use care in disposal of refuse and to take precautions against possible contamination of the water supply. Each party, upon vacating, is requested to put out his fire with water, remove all his tents or shelters and pick up all the rubbish.

These Camp Sites are all located along well traveled roads, trails and streams, and handy to a supply of water.

The Maine Highway Department will supply maps which show the location of these to any interested party.

Whenever you camp, be sure your fire is out before you leave.

A good many fires could be avoided if the smoker would only stop to think and see that his match, cigarette, cigar stub or pipe ashes is entirely out.

The forests are the greatest heritage that was ever given to the people of Maine. It is hoped that smokers and fishermen will always be mindful of helping to keep them green. When fires destroy the forests around the head waters of small trout streams the little spring feeders dry up and many trout die for want of water.

Broken bottles or broken glass left in the woods by picnic parties and transients can develop a cause of forest fires. Curved pieces of glass intensify the rays of the sun shining on them to the point where fire can ignite the dry leaves, duff or humus beneath.

The best time to stop a forest fire is just before you start it. A Fire-Proof forest demands one-hundred percent public cooperation. Wild Life depends on the forests. Keep Them Green.

Deer with horns in velvet.
Buck deer shed their horns every year in winter and new horns start growing in early spring. These new horns are soft and the outer surface looks like velvet.

Chapter 37

Where and When To Go Hunting and Fishing

If you want to go deer hunting in Maine you will find a map on the inside back cover of this Book showing where every deer was shot last year (1941). Write the Maine Publicity Bureau, 3 St. John St., Portland, Me. for **detail** information about the section that interests you. Ask them when the first snow is expected and be on the spot when it comes. Of course you may miss the snow but at that time of year the leaves are well off and you are almost sure to get **rain** or snow so that you can get around quietly. The weather will be much better for keeping game than earlier in the season. If you **do** get a light snow fall, without crust, hunting conditions will be perfect.

This is the best load of game seen passing through Freeport, Me., last Fall 1941. (A bear, 4 deer and a wild cat).

Fishing

If you want to go fishing in Maine, a great deal depends on the time you can get away. As a general rule the later in the season the further North you will need to go. For example Sebago Lake is fair fishing up to June 15th. Moosehead Lake is very fair up to August 1st and Rangeley Lakes are about in between. If you go later than August 1st you should pick your location very carefully. You may find it necessary to go way back on small streams or ponds.

Write the Maine Publicity Bureau the date you want to go and the makeup of your party. There are a number of places where you can get fair fishing right up until the season closes, but the chances are you will be obliged to do quite a great deal of walking.

When writing the Maine Publicity Bureau, insist on detail information regarding the section of the State in which you are interested.

Chapter 38—Your Guide

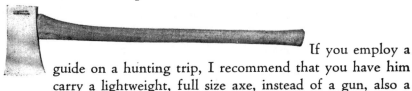

If you employ a guide on a hunting trip, I recommend that you have him carry a lightweight, full size axe, instead of a gun, also a

Photo—Courtesy Maine Inland Fisheries and Game Dept.
Veteran Beaver Trapper and Guide Jasper Haynes, on the right, with beaver trap showing how it is placed on pole under ice.
Note poplar stick used as bait tied to large pole.

A lightweight axe and a small pack sack with food and dishes for two people for three meals weighs only about 12 lbs.

very small pack sack with food enough for three meals, tin dishes for two, a small pail for making tea and a small fry pan.

In case of accident or other reasons you are obliged to stay out over night you will find one gun and one axe much better than two guns.

With an axe you can build a lean-to, get wood and make a fairly comfortable bed. In 1926 I was Caribou hunting in a very cold country. My guide carried an axe instead of a gun, also the other things mentioned above. We had a good hot meal every day at noon time. I was so impressed with the idea I have never allowed my guide to carry a gun since except to help hunt down a wounded deer. Years ago when my guide carried a gun duck hunting I never knew who shot the ducks. Now the guide attends to the sculling and I handle the gun. If a duck drops I know who shot it.

L. L. Bean (at left) and his hunting partner, L. P. Swett of Bangor, Me., with Caribou shot winter 1926.

You may be invited to make a party of four who make a practice of having cocktails, playing cards in camp and letting the guide shoot the deer. Don't accept the invitation. Learn to shoot your own deer. It will be a great deal more satisfactory. The open air and exercise is well worth your time even if you fail to get your deer.

The State of Maine has Class A and Class B Guides. The Inland Fish and Game laws provide, that "No person shall be issued a Class A guide's certificate unless he is physically, mentally and morally capable of guiding and caring for a party anywhere in the forests or on the waters of the State."

Chapter 39
General Information

When on your hunting trips do not try to belittle the back woods folk even though you are a college man and your home in a big city.

While your education and personal appearance may be far superior to theirs, they may be getting just as much pleasure out of life as yourself and when it comes right down to country common sense, they probably have you beaten.

A few years ago a New Jersey nimrod, while fishing in Northern Maine got mixed up in his direction while attempting a short-cut to camp. He finally ran into a barefoot boy and started asking him questions without admitting the fact that he did not know the way home. Unable to get an intelligent reply that would help him out of his predicament he finally said, "I guess you don't know much anyway, do you?" The boy answered, "No, but I'm not lost."

Photo—Courtesy Maine Inland Fisheries and Game Dept.

Jasper Haynes, Maine Trapper, skinning a beaver just pulled out of a trap through the ice.

You may be the big toad in the puddle when you are at home but don't try to poke fun at the "Small Town" folk until you are sure you are "out of the woods."

There are about twenty-three million fishermen, exclusive of commercial fishermen and about eight million hunters in the United States. Therefore, when you go fishing or hunting do not set your expectations too high. You may fish all day and not get a strike. You may hunt all day and not even see a deer. In fact you may go home empty-handed. Therefore, make up your mind to have a good time. Enjoy camp life and exercise in the open air and you will be well repaid for your trip. I have hunted three days without seeing a deer. On the fourth day I had my deer hung up and was spoting a trail back to camp before 9 A. M.

To be a successful hunter or fisherman you must have a great deal of patience.

Veteran Fox and Bobcat Trapper with four Cats trapped in one week on the road from Greenville to Chesuncook, Maine. The State of Maine will not only thank you but will pay $15.00 for shooting one of these deer-killers.

Chapter 40
Atlantic Salmon Fishing

The Atlantic Salmon is without doubt the scrappiest fish that can be taken on a fly. They are caught to some extent in Maine but at present the choicest fishing is in the eastern provinces of Canada and in Newfoundland.

The Atlantic Salmon migrate from the sea to the cold rivers to

Taking five salmon in a single day, L. L. Bean of Freeport Saturday broke the record for the famous Plaster Rock pool on the Tobique River in New Brunswick. Mr. Bean, shown above with his record day's catch, also set another unusal record by taking each fish on a different pattern of salmon fly. The fish, which weighed from 8½ to 9½ pounds each, were all landed on a 5½ ounce rod.

(Reproduced from Portland Sunday Telegram — June 15, 1941)

Mrs. J. Larry Hawks with two nice Atlantic Salmon.

spawn but unlike their Pacific brothers they do not die afterwards and often live to ten years during which time they will spawn as many as three times. The salmon always returns to the same river where he was hatched.

Nothing but fly fishing is permitted in the rivers. Contrary to general belief no fancy or special tackle is necessary. Your stiff fly rod and your ordinary fly line will do nicely except that you should splice fifty yards of 18 pound test backing on the line and have a reel large enough to carry it.

Numerous salmon flies are offered but the most popular are Jock Scott, Durham Ranger, Silver Doctor, Dusty Miller and Silver Gray in the order listed. The camp where you are staying usually supply the gaff or net.

Fishing can be done by wading, but on larger rivers, the canoe is more popular as it can be poled up stream and more water can be covered on the way down. A guide is necessary to handle the canoe.

Plenty of time should be taken in fishing so all the water is covered as a salmon's eyesight is none too good and they will seldom strike when further than six feet from the fly.

Salmon fishing differs from trout fishing in one important respect in that under no circumstances should you hold a looped line in the left hand while the fly is on the water. If you do and a salmon strikes he will either tear the fly out or break your leader. There will be no doubt about it when he strikes and no effort should be made to "horse" him in for you simply cannot do it.

While some fishermen prefer the early mornings and late evenings for salmon fishing just as many fish have been hooked at mid-day. Like other fish they take more readily on a changing temperature which always follows a rise or fall of the water.

Unlike most fish, salmon will not always strike a fly on the first cast. The author knows of one case where seventy-two casts were made in one spot over a salmon before he took the fly.

If the fisherman prefers to equip himself with special salmon tackle, I recommend a seven or eight ounce rod with a detachable butt. A triple tapered line of the "Bug Taper" variety with one hundred yards of eighteen pound test backing line. A reel with drag and large enough to hold the extra line. Leaders should be at least nine feet long and test about 10 lbs. A landing net about 17″ x 18″ at top and 36″ deep with handle six feet long.

Chapter 41   Canoeing

The most practical canoe for Maine Lakes and general canoe trips is the 20 ft. Guide model.

If you intend to use your canoe on swift water as well as lakes and ponds, a twenty-foot Guide's Model is best. If the canoe is to be used only on lakes and ponds, a canoe of the same size with a keel is preferable.

Two paddles, one 5½ feet long and the other 6 feet are necessary. Use paddles of seasoned maple or ash with well-shaped blade and shank.

For quick-water work you should have a good spruce pole 11 or 12 feet long and 2 inches in diameter, equipped with an iron socket on one end. A sponge for removing water and about 30 feet of strong clothesline is almost a necessity.

The pole is indispensable for going up swift streams where a paddle is useless. For going down stream, a pole is necessary to snub the canoe.

When going up a very fast stream where a pole cannot be used, attach one end of the clothesline to the bow of the canoe and walk along the bank of the stream and tow the craft as best you can. Let your companion keep the bow off shore with the aid of the pole. There are many streams too swift for the proper use of a line, necessitating carrying the canoe around such rapids. Before using a canoe in quick water, fill it with water and let it soak for an hour or two. A canoe that is very dry is apt to be brittle.

Photo—Courtesy Maine Inland Fisheries and Game Dept.

Warden Bert Duty poling over a dam on Mud Pond Stream, Maine.

The best way to learn how to properly handle a canoe is to go canoeing with a person who is familiar with such a craft. You will learn how to handle the bow paddle first, then the stern, and later the use of a pole. If you don't have an instructor, I suggest that for practice purposes you put two or three rocks in the bow. The total weight of the rocks should be at least 100 pounds. Choose a calm day for your first few practice lessons, and stay on a lake, pond or river where there is only a little current.

Paddle in easy, steady strokes, with one hand just above the blade and the other on the handle. Don't try to reach out too far and attempt to make extra-long strokes. Steering a canoe without paddling on one side and then the other is mastered by a little practice.

You can go down many streams without using a pole, but I do not suggest it unless you know the streams well and also are aware of all hidden rocks and sunken logs that might capsize your canoe if hit.

Take good care of your canoe. Don't push or pull a canoe around on the beach the way some folks handle rowboats. Carry a repair kit and examine your canoe daily while in use and repair all rips and tears.

Balancing of load in the canoe is very important. The heaviest of duffle must of necessity be in the center.

In running white water the load should balance slightly in back of center to allow the canoe to be swung or set instantly.

Chapter 42
Salt Water Fishing

I should not consider my book complete without a word about Salt Water Fishing.

Mrs. L. L. Bean and 8 ft. Sail Fish caught by her at Palm Beach, Florida, February 14, 1941.

In recent years, Maine has added salt water fishing for giant bluefin tuna, striped bass and mackerel.

The best spot for tuna fishing is in the Bailey Island area of Casco Bay where these giant fish run from 200 lbs. up to over 700.

Regulation big game, deep sea fishing outfits are necessary to handle these giant bluefins, with the minimum tackle being 16 oz. tips, at least 500 yards of 24-thread line, and 10/0 reel.

For the beginner I recommend 36-thread line and a 14/0 reel, also that you hire a regular fishing boat that is fully equipped for taking out parties. After fishing for a season or two, you might want to own your own boat. The best season is late July to mid-September. Due to recent increases in striped bass, anglers have found that Maine can produce plenty of activity for the thousands of salt water anglers who look upon striped bass as one of the finest light tackle salt water fish. One of the most reliable lures for stripers is the sea-worm, (sometimes called blood worm) either with or without sinker or spinner or trolling with a smooth running spinner baited with sea-worms. Although most of Maine's best striped bass fishing is in the tidal waters of its streams, these fish can also be taken surf casting, and here a regulation surf-casting outfit is in order. Best season is from late June through September.

Another form of salt water fishing that has gained great favor with fly fishermen is fly fishing for mackerel. Although small, seldom exceeding a pound in weight, these trim torpedoes strike eagerly at streamer and bucktail flies and, "ounce for ounce," are worthy of the skill of any fly fisherman.

"Clinch Knot" For Fishing Leaders

One of the best known knots for nylon leaders is illustrated at

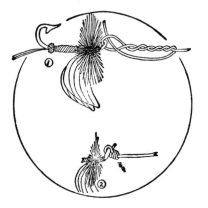

the left. Stick the end of the tippet through the eye of the fly, double it back against itself for four or five inches, give the fly several complete twists to wind the leader spirally around itself four or five times as shown in Figure I.

Thrust the end between the eye and the coils, hold on to it, and pull up tightly and securely as shown in Figure II.

The Following Are Extracts From Maine Laws

Bear

Bear traps shall be plainly labeled with the full name and address of the person setting the same and must be enclosed in a hut, or by at least two strands of barbed wire, one four and one five feet from the ground, said wire to be securely held in position and to be not less than five yards at any point from the enclosed trap.

Deer

No person shall at any time in any manner transport or move any deer or part thereof unless open to view and there is securely attached thereto a tag bearing the name and address of the person who killed said deer and it shall be accompanied by him while being transported.

Public Camp Sites

"Non-Residents shall not kindle fires upon any unorganized township, while engaged in camping, fishing or hunting from May first to December first, without being in charge of a registered guide, except at public camp sites maintained by the forestry department. No guide shall at the same time guide or be employed by more than five non-residents in hunting."

Wild Animals

I have received a number of letters asking if I were ever chased by a bear or charged by a bull moose.

In all my experience hunting and fishing in Maine and Canada, I have never been attacked by a wild animal.

While I have heard several stories about hunters being treed by bear and moose I have never known of one authentic case.

Summer Care of Snowshoes

Wipe clean and varnish both the wood and webbing. Any high grade spar-varnish will do. Two coats are better than one, but in any case they should be thin coats.

Tie the shoes securely together, back to back, and force block of wood into the space between the toes.

Place them out of the sun and hang by the tail. Suspend by wire so that mice or squirrels cannot get at them.

Chapter 43
Baxter State Park

Percival P. Baxter and Garry

While I have made this book primarily one of practical information for hunting, fishing and camping, I cannot close without a brief chapter on Maine's unspoiled wilderness reservation, and the State's greatest benefactor, former Governor Percival P. Baxter, the man who literally has given away mountains.

Here in the heart of Maine, 145 miles north of Bangor, this modest man has realized a long cherished ambition to preserve in its primeval ruggedness the State's natural heritage of rugged beauty in the Katahdin region which embraces 30 or more mountain peaks including the lofty Katahdin range.

After fifteen years of planning and negotiation he brought about the accomplishment of his dream, to give to his beloved native State of Maine this vast tract of wilderness, which in his own words should "remain the wild storm-swept, untouched-by-man region it now is; that is its great charm."

Chimney Pond and the East wall of Katahdin.

Photo—Courtesy Portland Press Herald

Pamola Peak (4902 feet) on the left and Baxter Peak on the right with the knife edge between. At the center is the chimney, granite-walled gorge leading down the mountain. The knife edge, in places, is only a few feet wide.

This vast area covering almost five townships is filled with dense forests, rugged mountain peaks, quiet ponds, sparkling lakes, deep gorges and broad valleys.

In the midst of it all rises Baxter Peak on the Katahdin range of its lofty height within twelve to fifteen feet of a mile above sea level. This is truly a majestic sight, one of nature's great masterpieces.

Where in all the world can be found such an inviting paradise for hikers, campers, mountain climbers and those who love the great outdoors where nature abounds unspoiled by man?

This vast natural park of 112,945 acres of land (see map inside front cover) is a veritable wild life sanctuary where beast and bird thrive unmolested. Here you may see beaver dams making lakes of 50 acres or more. In truth more wild life can be found here than in any other part of Maine. And so it will remain, thanks to Percival P. Baxter, whose generosity has made this great natural park both a possibility and a reality for this and all future generations.

Photo—Courtesy Maine Development Commission
Baxter Camp and Katahdin stream on the West side of Baxter Park.

Photo—Courtesy Maine Development Commission

**Pinnacle Rock on the West side of
Mt. Katahdin, Baxter Park.**

Hunting is forbidden and fishing only is allowed in season, for in Percival Baxter's deeds of gift to the State, it is provided that "the said land shall forever be used by said State for **State Forest, Public Park and Public Recreational Purposes, Shall Forever Be Left In Its Natural Wild State, and Shall Forever Be Kept as a Sanctuary for Wild Beasts and Birds.**" Only small cabins for mountain climbers and those who love the wilderness are allowed.

Mr. Baxter in his own words says, "As modern civilization with its trailers and gasoline fumes, its unsightly billboards,

Katahdin Campsite at the foot of Hunt Trail, Baxter Park.

its radio and jazz, encroaches on the Maine wilderness, the time yet may come when only the Katahdin region remains undefiled by man. To acquire this Katahdin region for the people of Maine was undertaken by me as my life's work, and I hope as the years roll on, that this State Park will be enjoyed by an ever-increasing number of Maine people and by those who come to us from beyond our borders."

Thus, not only to the citizens of Maine has been dedicated this natural monument to the everlasting memory of our former Governor, but also to the people of an entire nation has been established a reservation where they may glory in the rugged aspects of nature and where wild life may dwell in peace without fear of gun, trap, or other human encroachment.

Within the borders of this great natural Park are 40 lakes, ponds and deadwaters, also innumerable streams and brooks. With negligible exceptions, they are all open to fishing.

There are several camp sites in the Park. One of the camp sites at the foot of the Hunt Trail, is known as the Katahdin Campsite. It is right on the road that runs from Millinocket to Greenville. This road is travelled very little and while not first class it is adequate. This camp site will accommodate at least 100 campers.

Photo—Courtesy Maine Inland Fisheries and Game Dept.

One of the many Beaver Dams in Baxter Park.

The State has built at this spot 30 shelters like the picture on page 93. These are available to campers at a price of fifteen cents per day to cover the cost of maintenance. Although open on one side, they are located so that wind and rain doesn't bother. There is, in addition, room for quite a few tents in this beautiful spot.

It is known that it is Mr. Baxter's ambition to continue adding to this great Park until it covers six townships, making the total area 144,000 square acres. This will take out all notches shown in map on inside front cover of this book. When this is accomplished the Park will be oblong (18 miles long and 12 miles wide).

Photo—Courtesy Maine Development Commission

Chimney Pond Lean-to, Baxter Park.

It is also known that Mr. Baxter has included in his will a bequest of sufficient funds to maintain it.

For detail information in regard to camping, hiking and fishing write the Maine Publicity Bureau, 3 St. John Street, Portland, Maine.

Cut Out The Five Following Chapters To Keep On Your Person When Big Game Hunting

Duplicate Chapter 3
How To Dress A Deer

First swing him around so that his head will hang over a small log or nubble with hind quarters down hill. Spread his hind legs well apart, make a careful incision in the belly right where it curves up from the legs, cutting through the skin and the very thin layer covering the paunch. Remembering that the hide and membrane is very thin here and that you do not want to cut into the paunch. Place the point of your knife between the first two fingers of your left hand, so that the back of the hand will press the paunch down and the point of the knife will cut the skin. Cut forward until you have an opening from twelve to fifteen inches long. Roll up both sleeves above the elbow, insert both hands, one on each side of the paunch, well forward and roll it out through the opening. Do not make this opening any larger than is necessary in order to do this. The bowels and liver will follow the paunch. Now reach way forward with your right hand and you will strike a membranous wall. Puncture this with your fingers and on the other side you will find his heart and lungs. Reach beyond this and cut windpipe with jackknife. Now pull out the heart and lungs and you have a deer that is known as "woods dressed". It is not necessary to cut the throat to bleed him. In most cases all the blood will escape through the shot hole. If not, the dressing operation will bleed him thoroughly. It is a good idea to remove the end of the intestine at the rectum. By doing this you will make a drain. By drawing a small bough through this hole all the blood will drain out.

Duplicate Chapter 4
How To Hang Up A Deer

If a small one you will have no trouble as you can tie your drag line around his neck, throw the loose end over the limb of a tree and pull him clear of the ground.

If a big deer, find a sapling that can be pulled over so that you can hitch your line to it high enough so that when it springs back it will lift the carcass from the ground. In case the "spring back" is not enough, use a pole with crotch or fork at end to prop it back in place.

In some cases two poles are much better than one. Now sign and detach tag from your hunting license and fasten it to the deer.

The next thing is to spot (blaze) trees and bushes from where it is hung to the nearest travelled trail or stream that leads to camp.

Do not depend on your memory as to where the deer is hung. Many a deer has never been found after it was hung up.

Dragging a big buck on bare ground for several miles is a task that you will long remember. Get all the members of your party to help you.

If you kill a deer "way back" and can hire someone with a horse to transport it to camp, you certainly are in luck, because the few dollars that you spend for toting will save you much hard labor.

Duplicate Chapter 14
Signals For Hunters

It is very important that you have a system of signals that every member of your party will recognize. I recommend the following: When you want to get in touch with another member fire two shots about five seconds apart. Anyone of your party hearing it will reply with two shots. You answer with one shot. He immediately starts looking for you. After traveling ten minutes he will fire one shot and you will answer with one. When he believes that he is near you, he will "Hello." Not receiving an answer he will fire one more shot which you will answer with one. Continue this one shot conversation until you are within hailing distance. After calling for help and receiving a reply **do not** leave your position.

Duplicate Chapter 15
How To Use A Compass

There is no excuse for getting lost if you carry a good compass and know how to use it.

Camping places are invariably located on trail, tote road, stream, lake, telephone wire, etc. We will say that your camp is on a good sized stream or well defined road running North and South. You cross the stream or road and hunt to the East for several hours. When you want to go to camp all you need to do is travel West. Hold compass so needle arrow points to "N" then pick out some object in a due West direction and go to it. Keep repeating this and you are sure to hit your road but it may be a mile or more below or above your camp. You are out of the woods anyway and if you have been over the road a few times you will soon see land marks that will tell you which way to go.

Lakes, old railroads, telephone wires, etc., always run in some general direction and you must be sure of this direction when you start out and always be sure which side you are hunting on.

Before starting out I usually get someone in the party to help make a rough sketch of the territory and always carry it with me. A rough map of this kind is a big help to find the very shortest way to camp.

At times you will feel sure your compass is wrong. The best way to overcome this feeling is to carry two compasses. In checking one compass against the other, place them eight or ten feet apart and away from your gun or other metal. Another reason for carrying two compasses is that one might get broken. In fact compasses have been known to get out of order. When compass needle swings back and forth several times and finally settles in the same direction on two or three tests it is O. K.

(cut along this line)

Duplicate Chapter 16
How To Find A Lost Hunter

In case one of your party does not show up when night falls as has previously been his custom, do not get excited and do not do a thing until 6:00 P. M. If you start signaling before 6:00 P. M. other hunters who have not gotten into camp are likely to butt in and make it very misleading.

Eat your supper and see that the lantern is full of oil. Then go outside with rifle, lantern and flashlight. At exactly 6:00 P. M. fire two shots. Listen a moment for a reply. Not hearing any, walk about one-quarter mile and repeat your signal. If you get a reply, see a fire or note any odor of smoke, continue the signals, always walking in the general direction that you believe your man is located.

In the meantime what is the "lost" hunter to do? If, in the late afternoon, he realizes that he is lost or so far from camp that he cannot get in, he selects a sheltered spot where dry wood is handy, starts a fire and collects a lot of wood before dark. At exactly 6:00 P. M. he listens for a signal. On hearing it, he answers and the signals continue the same as in the daytime. Hearing no signal he wastes none of his shells but pounds a signal at regular intervals with a club on a sound, dead tree. If there is no dead tree available, he selects a live tree and peels off a spot of bark where he wants to pound.

In the morning, if not sure of the direction to camp, he is not to leave the spot or to shoot except to answer his party's signals. Keep a smoke going and pound out a few signals about every ten minutes.

The party at camp should not stay out too late. Notify a Game Warden or Sheriff during the night and continue the search at daybreak.

By following these simple rules the lost hunter or his party has nothing to worry about.

Date

Party Consisted of

Went To

Game Shot - Fish Caught

Hunting - Fishing Conditions

Neglected to Take

Didn't Use

Notes

Date

Party Consisted of

Went To

Game Shot - Fish Caught

Hunting - Fishing Conditions ....

....

Neglected to Take ....

....

Didn't Use ....

....

Notes ....

Date ....

Party Consisted of ....

....

Went To ....

Game Shot - Fish Caught ....

....

Hunting - Fishing Conditions ....

....

Neglected to Take ....

....

Didn't Use ....

....

Notes ....

....

....

Date ....

Party Consisted of ....

....

Went To ....

Game Shot - Fish Caught ....

....

Hunting - Fishing Conditions ....

....

Neglected to Take ....

....

Didn't Use ....

....

Notes ....

==

Date ....

Party Consisted of ....

....

Went To ....

Game Shot - Fish Caught ....

....

....

Hunting - Fishing Conditions ....

....

Neglected to Take ....

....

Didn't Use ....

....

Notes ....

Date ....

Party Consisted of ....

....

Went To ....

Game Shot - Fish Caught ....

....

Hunting - Fishing Conditions ....

....

Neglected to Take ....

....

Didn't Use ....

....

Notes ....

....

....

Date..

Party Consisted of...

....

Went To..

Game Shot - Fish Caught..

....

Hunting - Fishing Conditions...

....

Neglected to Take..

....

Didn't Use...

....

Notes..

....

Date..

Party Consisted of...

....

Went To..

Game Shot - Fish Caught..

....

....

Hunting - Fishing Conditions ....

....

Neglected to Take ....

....

Didn't Use ....

....

Notes ....

Date ....

Party Consisted of ....

....

Went To ....

Game Shot - Fish Caught ....

....

Hunting - Fishing Conditions ....

....

Neglected to Take ....

....

Didn't Use ....

....

Notes ....

....

....